MAŻE *The* MAGAŻINE

An A-Z storehouse of expertise for living in love

By

John and Sue Roseblade

Welcome!

©FreeImages.com/Piotr Lewandowski

Welcome to THE MAGAZINE!

For many couples, when the fireworks of first attraction have fizzled out, the effort involved in pursuing the dream of a deeply satisfying togetherness seems an impossible task. We would love you to prove this assumption wrong as you embark on the exciting adventure that we are setting before you.

We are a very ordinary couple with experiences similar to many of yours. By God's daily grace we have raised four children and scraped through many challenges. Gradually our rough edges are being smoothed, and we are daring to recognise and accept our real selves as well as each other. Our capacity for true love is increasing as our understanding continues to grow.

Just as a healthy diet will fail to keep us in trim if we return to our old eating habits, so we have had to recognise that the development of our emotional and relational skills is only effective in as much as we continue to put into practice what we learn, and allow both our successes and our mistakes to make us more mature in our characters.

By learning to exercise more loving attitudes, many people find that they grow to love themselves better. Hopefully, if this happens for you, and you begin to enjoy the new you that emerges, you won't want to allow old habits to return.

Our passion is to support and encourage all those of you who want to know that you are not alone in your struggles and it is our great delight to offer you the hope of rekindling your first love as you engage with the activities in THE MAGAZINE.

©iStockphoto.com/ddsign_stock

You will need an hour or so each week: in a place, and at a time, that works for both of you. Try to make it a stress free, technology free zone, enhanced by coffee and cake, or whatever favourite treats you enjoy, so that you will look forward to it eagerly and not allow it to get sidelined. If you make a strong commitment to one another to prioritise these times together you will be able to pursue your goals consistently, deliberately and systematically and you will see the impossible begin to happen!

Our thoughts and our prayers are with you,

John and Sue

About...

Why Invest In The Magazine?

From recent statistics, as well as our own conclusions, it appears that sticking together in today's culture isn't as easy as ABC! The evidence is all around us and our whole society is affected by the hurt, damage and financial hardships that result from broken families. If the formula for being happy in a relationship was as simple as learning to read or write, we would all be experts.

However, our own experience is that since we were married in 1978 we are still learning on a daily basis and, whether you have been together for five months or fifty years, no doubt you are still learning too! It was only after 28 years together that we first went on a relationship course. We had considered that we had a good marriage, but what we learned about each other through the course was a huge milestone in developing it from good to better. Since then we have seen the value of continually setting time aside to talk and reinvest.

Thus, THE MAGAZINE is as much a project for our own benefit as for yours, but we wanted to pass on to you the essence of what we can all enjoy through learning to connect at a deeper level. We hope that as you take part in the activities on each page, your energy levels will rise and your enthusiasm for life will bring a new sparkle to your eyes!

Our objective is to provide a resource that gives couples a formula for educating themselves, in a workshop style format, that is regular, interactive, private, non-threatening, inexpensive and easily accessible in the comfort of their own home.

©iStockphoto.com/3dts

"Marriage education workshops can make a real difference in helping married couples stay together and in encouraging unmarried couples who are living together to form a more lasting bond."

BARACK OBAMA 2006

©FreeImages.com/Vinicius Sgarbe

©FreeImages.com/Shalom Pennington

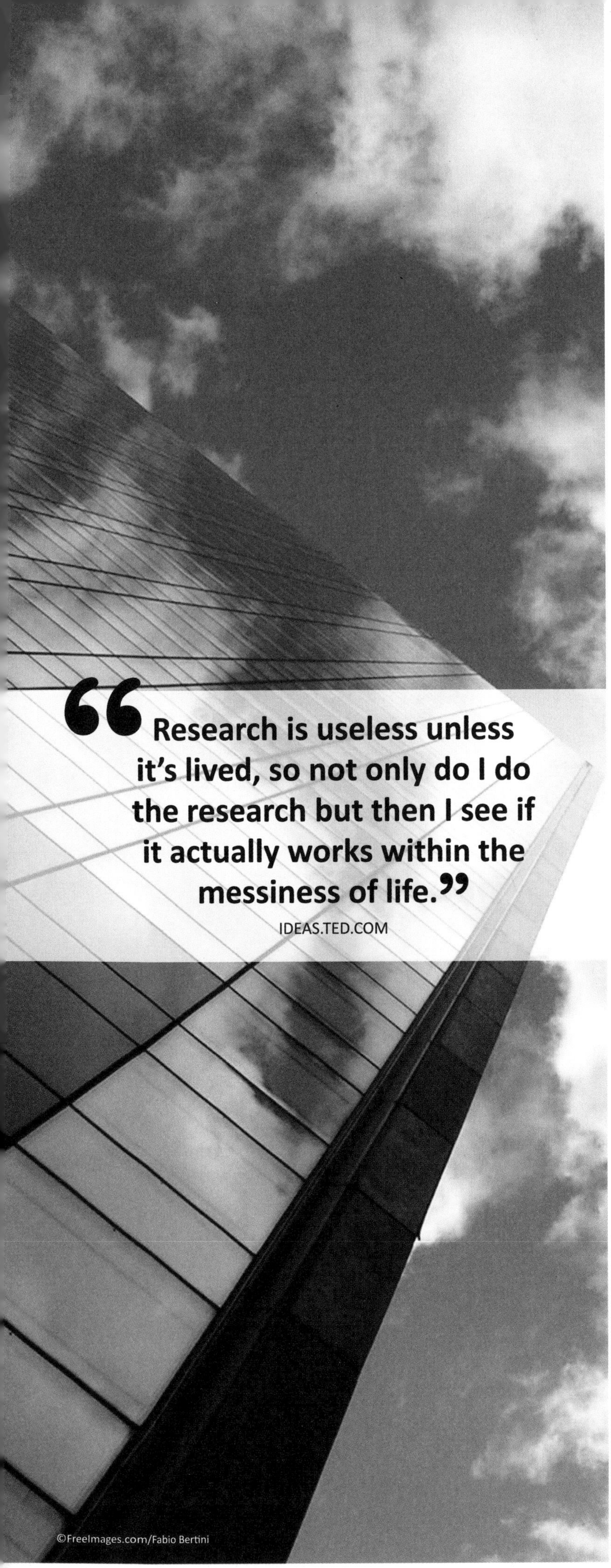

What's T[illegible]

Although, for u[illegible] made to the [illegible] of marriage [illegible] understand [illegible] embarking [illegible] THE MAGAZI[illegible] differently. Ple[illegible] rather than husbands and wives, forgive the more traditional elements of our terminology. We recognise that times are changing and we long that the material we have put together will be accessible to all of you, whatever particular faith or position you may hold. You will, however, through these pages see how we have found two things to be true for us.

Firstly, we have found the Bible to be a great storehouse of wisdom for making our marriage happier and healthier. Secondly, the vows we made to one another, in front of family, friends and God, have been a great strength and an anchor through the more testing times. More than anything else, these two elements of our experience of commitment lead us to be very cautious about not throwing the baby of marriage out with the bath water of 21st century culture.

Our hope is to give you food for thought, but to be very down-to-earth at the same time. The stories and challenges are all very practical examples and tasks, with which we know you will identify. We have avoided majoring on the impact of faith in developing healthy relationships, even though, for us, knowing Jesus is the transforming power we rely on as we live daily with the mission we are inviting you to undertake. If, through what you read in THE MAGAZINE, you are challenged and motivated to look into finding out more about how the Christian faith impacts relationships, please go to the rear section of THE MAGAZINE entitled "The Megazone". On pages 126-129 you will find an article called "Gravity and Groundwork" which you may find relevant and interesting. Our desire is simply to pass on what has worked for us. So, please, take what you can from our material, and forgive us the rest.

We have found the following to be the key to our making progress: "Research is useless unless it's lived, so not only do I do the research but then I see if it actually works within the messiness of life." IDEAS.TED.COM

So, here is the research done in the middle of our mess!

How Has The Magazine Come About?

THE MAGAZINE has been developed as a follow up to our one day course, MAZE, so that couples can continue to pay attention to the health of their relationship on a weekly basis. Both these projects are intended as opportunities for taking some time out of the busy routine of life in order to look afresh at our relationships. MAZE was given its title because pursuing togetherness can be like walking through a complicated maze with numerous twists and turns and many blind alleys. It aims to offer some key tactics that will help in the lifelong process of discovering our own route through to the central heart of relationship.

Feedback from MAZE has led us to write THE MAGAZINE as a means of maintaining the momentum gained on the day course throughout the year. In addition to its more common meaning today, the term magazine originally meant 'a store' and is often used when referring to a military stash of arms or ammunition. We hope it will become a storehouse of wisdom and a treasury of opportunities for you to draw from that will help you to mature in loving one another.

There is no need to have attended a MAZE day before setting out to use THE MAGAZINE, but it may be well worth considering booking a course as a springboard before you embark on this weekly version of the project. Our website address is to be found on the back cover and we would be pleased to discuss setting up a MAZE day for a few couples in your area or to hear any feedback you would like to give us about your experience of using THE MAGAZINE.

Where Do We Begin?

If you are keen to get started, here are some important tips on how to make the most of THE MAGAZINE:

MAKING THE MOST OF THE PROJECT

- Agree to spend an hour each week engaging in one of the weekly missions.
- Ideally have a copy each so that you can enter your own jottings and reminders.
- Put the needs of the relationship above your own needs.
- Recognise that the price of failure is always higher than the cost of perseverance.
- Choose to enter your soul mate's world.
- See the topics as non-threatening springboards for discussion.
- Recognise that we all have blind spots.
- Know that there are some simple keys to staying in love.
- See the good in each other and believe the best at all times.
- Be ready to forgive.

When's The Best Time?

The best time to begin anything new is straight away! Strike while the iron's hot! Agree a time in the week when you will both be most relaxed and can devote between thirty minutes and an hour to look at a topic.

Following The Layout

There are double page spreads for each letter of the alphabet and there are two activities (or missions) per letter. We suggest that you aim to work through one mission topic per week. As there are 26 letters in the alphabet and 52 weeks in a year, this will give you a focus for your relationship each week throughout a whole year. By the end of the year, you may well be ready to revisit some of the exercises and get even more from them!

We suggest that you use two consecutive weeks to do the two missions of a double page spread, because there is often a link between the topics they address. However, there is no need to cover all the letters in alphabetical order. You can pick and choose according to what you feel would benefit you most.

When you come to engage in your mission for the week, consider whether it is an activity for you to focus on together or one that is better done alone. Allow one another the space to process and work on any targets without putting each other under any time pressure. On the other hand, where conversation and sharing is instructed, do enter into this fully and enthusiastically in order to put as much as you can into the relationship. If one of you is much keener on talking than the other, it may be an idea to set a timer, so that the less talkative partner knows that there will be a definite time to conclude the conversation. That way, the idea of an in-depth discussion can be less threatening!

Finally Some Crucial Tips For Good Communication Skills:

THE MAGAZINE will only be effective in helping you to develop your relationship if you are able to communicate with each other. We hope that as you engage in each of the mission activities that your skills in speaking and listening will improve significantly.

In order to help you we have put together the following guidelines that will steer you towards a successful outcome to your discussions:

1. Be assertive – state what you feel and what you would like to happen clearly and politely, without apologies or confusing hints.
2. Be respectful – don't interrupt and use good manners at all times.
3. Stay focussed – listen attentively and don't allow yourself to get distracted.
4. Repeat what you hear – this involves responding by saying exactly what you have understood has been shared with you, rather than jumping in with your reactions or your defence. It will make the other person feel valued and understood.
5. Seek clarification – ask if what you have repeated back is a true interpretation of your partner's feelings and their meaning.

At the end of your discussion, assess whether you feel different:

a. towards each other

b. about the issue

So wherever you see this icon throughout THE MAGAZINE you can refer back to these guidelines before you begin your discussion.

Appreciation & Admiration

Message

Appreciation is a personal application of our attitude of gratitude. Often we can feel thankful for something, but not express our thanks in words. It can be easier to speak out our criticisms and disappointments rather than our thanks, and this leads us to take others for granted. Just because we are married to them, our spouse is not obliged to run round after us trying to meet all our needs. They will feel much more inclined to do some of their daily chores if we express our appreciation to them consistently and enthusiastically.

Maybe you began your relationship with a sense of admiration for the person you thought you were "falling in love with", only to wonder after some years together how they seem to have diminished in your estimation. Did they change or did you? It is usual that people will put their best qualities into a relationship during the "getting to know you" phase. Human beings love others to think well of them and will go above and beyond their normal behaviours in order to make a good impression, particularly in a new job or in the early stages of dating. However, once we become secure and comfortable in a setting, it is common for us to relax and difficult for us to keep up our best behaviour at all times. It is so much easier to display admirable qualities when we are being admired.

Micro Story

"I had been encouraging our teenage son to improve the way he kept his room. One day, having helped him to tidy his things away, I left him with the polish and duster. After about half an hour he called me to inspect his workmanship. My first impression was that he had done a really good job, but then I spotted a high shelf. The afternoon sun had moved round just far enough to highlight a lingering streak of dust. Without any thought for the consequences, I quickly drew his attention to the offending shelf, presuming that a simple wipe with the duster would rectify the problem and all would be well: but not so. He was mortified, and complained that, after all his hard work, I couldn't find a word of praise, only criticism. I learned that day to keep my perfectionist tendencies for my own character development, and to be more appreciative towards others."

Sue

Myth Or Truth?

A

If I praise and thank my spouse, they will become big headed.

If I praise and thank my spouse they will become more appreciative of me.

©dreamstime.com/Drawinglounge

©iStockphoto.com/KatarzynaBialasiewicz

Meditation

"One of the main reasons that we lose our enthusiasm in life is because we become ungrateful. We let what was once a miracle, become common to us. We get so accustomed to goodness it becomes a routine."
Joel Osteen, Your Best Life Now: 7 Steps to Living at Your Full Potential

"Feeling gratitude and not expressing it is like..... wrapping a present and not giving it."
William Arthur Ward

Imagine a scenario in which you are meeting your husband or wife again for the very first time and aim to recapture in your mind all the things that you first admired in them. Take time to enjoy how that makes you feel.

Mission "Gift Wrapped"

WEEK 1

Your mission is to move from aggravation to appreciation.

List 5 things your spouse does on a daily or weekly basis that you appreciate:

1

2

3

4

5

Focus this week on speaking out your thanks for these things giving specific reasons for your appreciation.

Thank you so much for keeping an eye on the bank account for us, otherwise it would be so easy for us to overspend. You are so much better with figures than I am.

WEEK 2

Your mission is to move from annoyance to admiration.

Ignoring all the things that annoy you, make a list of all the character traits you have ever seen as admirable in your spouse.

Focus on looking for every admirable thought, attitude or action your spouse demonstrates in the coming week, however minor, and compliment them on these qualities. Take every opportunity in conversation with others to mention something you admire in your spouse, speaking as their number one fan!

Tell your spouse about those conversations.

A

"This life is for loving, sharing, learning, smiling, caring, forgiving, laughing, hugging, helping, dancing, wondering, healing, and even more loving. I choose to live life this way. I want to live my life in such a way that when I get out of bed in the morning, the devil says, 'aw shute, he's up!"

Steve Maraboli, Unapologetically You: Reflections on Life and the Human Experience

Bridges & Balance

Meditation

You cannot push a ten tonne lorry of correction over a one tonne bridge of relationship.

Communication can build either barriers or bridges, depending on how you develop your skill.

Softening your communication skills will help your spouse to feel more comfortable, motivated, or appreciated. Do you lead slowly and gently into a contentious issue, or do you charge straight in with both feet?

“A soft answer turns away wrath, but a harsh word stirs up anger.”

Proverbs 15:1 RSV

“Communication is a continual balancing act, juggling the conflicting needs for intimacy and independence. To survive in the world, we have to act in concert with others, but to survive as ourselves, rather than simply as cogs in a wheel, we have to act alone.”

Deborah Tannen

Micro Story

One off the cuff remark:
a quarter century of imprisonment...

“At about the age of six I remember being at my aunt and uncle's house for a family tea. I was playing with my cousins, and an incident arose over the sharing of a toy. I have no idea whether or not I was to blame, but I clearly recall my mum telling me I was a selfish person. As an adult I have found self acceptance very difficult. It is only a few years ago that I finally understood how loving myself was not a selfish thing to do, and I have begun to be able to accept compliments and to develop a normal level of self esteem. I was always over sensitive to the slightest criticism and had become highly perfectionist about myself as a result. With my husband's patient and persevering love, I have been able to see that I don't need to defend myself or be right in every argument in order to protect my self image. Instead I can let these coping mechanisms go and I can be free to make mistakes, without feeling a complete failure.”

Lily

B

Message

Communication forms a bridge between us. The quality of the bridge will depend on how well we are able to communicate, and this will be determined by a number of factors. It will depend on:

..... our skill and perseverance in designing and building our bridge

..... the construction materials we have at our disposal

..... our willingness to make sure we have a maintenance programme in place

..... traumas that come along and thwart our efforts

Crossing the bridge of relationship that we establish through our communication can sometimes feel like walking a tightrope. We need an incredible degree of balance not to lose our footing. Often we can feel like we are treading on eggshells. Learning the art of balance is useful in every area of life, but never more so than in our communication. We need to speak and to listen. We need to understand and to be understood. We need to both express and to control our emotions.

Mission "What You Say Is What You Get"

WEEK 1

Your mission is to break down barriers and build your bridge.

Read through these soft lead in phrases which could all be used to initiate a conversation, and pick three you think would be useful for improving your bridge building skills:

- When you have a moment.....
- Can I ask you a question, please?
- So, what you're really feeling is.....
- I know you already told me this, but.....
- It's my fault we didn't.....
- I'm really interested in what you said about.....
- It would be so nice if we could.....
- How would you feel if.....
- Would it be helpful if I.....
- I don't mean to distract / interrupt you but.....
- Forgive me for not remembering, but.....
- I don't have all the answers, but.....

Start practising them this week!

Ask your husband or wife if you are in the habit of using any particular phrases that upset or annoy them and causes your communication to fall apart. You may not be aware of what they are – but your spouse can probably tell you!!!

Write them here and determine to eliminate them from your conversation:

____

____

____

____

____

____

____

____

WEEK 2

Your mission is to move away from communication breakdown towards balanced interaction.

Practise having a balanced conversation with your spouse. One of you begin the conversation by talking for about two minutes on the topic given below. Then afterwards the listener must reflect back to the speaker the essence of what they have said, particularly any feelings that have been expressed, in as much detail as they can recall. This reply should not involve giving any of your own opinions, but should be simply feeding back the message you heard in a way that affirms the speaker. Then swap roles.

Topic for discussion:

"What tensions do we experience between us when we are in the company of other people? How could we begin to overcome these issues?"

©iStockphoto.com/YinYang

©iStockphoto.com/aldegonde

©iStockphoto.com/julos

Husband to counsellor:

"No, I'm not worried about us drifting apart. I downloaded the GPS friend finding app to my phone!"

Myth Or Truth?

Sticks and stones may break my bones, but words will never hurt me.

"Most of us have a pretty total recall of things said to us in anger."

Libby Purves: How not to be a perfect family

©iStockphoto.com/kisgorcs

©FreeImages.com/Robert Owen-Wahl

Co-operation & Creativity

Message

Some people are competitive; some are not. Depending on how you were brought up, competing in games or sports may be very important to you. Developing an attitude that allows someone else to win, even when we are stronger or cleverer is a grace that some of us learn more easily than others. For many of us it only happens after becoming parents when we have to allow our children to beat us in their early attempts at lotto or dominoes. Voluntarily losing a game or an argument moves us from competitiveness to co-operation and we do well if we can find a healthy balance between the two.

Too competitive a spirit can mean that we are likely to belittle people. It may well be a symptom of an overinflated ego. This will not make for a healthy marriage.

Egotistic people can also fall prey to complacency. This is an attitude that is easy to adopt when life is going well. Our ego will try to tell us that it is to our own credit that everything is running smoothly. Strangely, the result of this belief is to relax and no longer to put in the energy the relationship requires. Complacency, therefore, is a self-defeating attitude which is very dangerous in a relationship. To counter it we need to be creative in finding ways to keep our love alive.

Micro Story

“After the birth of our first son we found competitiveness crept into our relationship. It began because our days were suddenly very different with me being at home with a baby while my husband worked to support us. I felt I wanted my husband to understand that being at home wasn't an 'easy ride'. I worried that he would think I just spent my days out for coffee with friends, spending money he'd worked hard for. As a result each day he would come home and I would tell him all the bad or hard bits about my day and he would remind me that working wasn't a walk in the park either. Gradually this became a daily download and it was only when one day he came home fifteen minutes late and said that he hadn't felt like coming straight home from work that I was suddenly aware of what it was doing to our marriage. I was saddened that he'd rather stay at work a few more minutes than come home to us because I'd made home an unappealing place to be. We had to step back and appreciate each other's perspective. I had to remember that working is not easy and tell him that I appreciated him supporting us financially and that I was grateful to be able to be home with our baby. In return he explained that he understood that being at home with a child wasn't easy but that he loved us and wanted to come home and hear all the good things about our day. What a difference! Whenever I feel the temptation to complain about my day, I now try instead to put myself in his shoes and show him appreciation for what he does for us and he comes home at lunchtime and straight from work to be with us because it's where he loves to be.”

Karen

Meditation

Spend a few minutes thinking about the contrasting views of these two sportsmen:

"Anyone who imagines they can work alone, winds up surrounded by nothing but rivals, without companions. The fact is, no one ascends alone."

Lance Armstrong, It's Not About the Bike: My Journey Back to Life

"I play to win, whether during practice or a real game. And I will not let anything get in the way of me and my competitive enthusiasm to win."

Michael Jordan – basketball player

Have you ever stopped to think about how someone who is very competitive makes other people feel? If you have, you are probably not very competitive yourself, if not, then you probably are!

Ask yourself how competitive your husband or wife would say you are and think about how this is affecting THEIR self esteem.

Mission "Losers or Winners"

WEEK 1

Your mission is to move from competition to co-operation.

Assess yourself on a scale of 1-10 in terms of how competitive you think you are: (circle below: 1 = not very / 10 = very)

1 2 3 4 5 6 7 8 9 10

In order to gauge this more accurately, answer the following questions on the same scale of 1-10:

- How likely would you be to let a five year old beat you at a board game?

1 2 3 4 5 6 7 8 9 10

- How likely would you be to beat a sports opponent week after week, even though you could see they were getting despondent?

1 2 3 4 5 6 7 8 9 10

- How likely would you be to make sure that the spread of chores between you and your husband or wife worked out fairly in an average week?

1 2 3 4 5 6 7 8 9 10

- To what extent would you expect your husband or wife to take over some of your tasks if you hadn't slept well?

1 2 3 4 5 6 7 8 9 10

- Now ask your husband or wife to what extent they agree with the way you have rated yourself!

1 2 3 4 5 6 7 8 9 10

Write one way in which you could be more co-operative instead of competitive that would help your marriage:

WEEK 2

Your mission is to move from complacency to creativity.

Fill in the boxes below with any ways in which you think you might take your life or your marriage for granted.

I take it for granted that.....

I take it for granted that.....

I take it for granted that.....

I take it for granted that.....

I take it for granted that.....

I take it for granted that.....

Now pick one box that you have filled in and think creatively about what you could do in order not to be complacent about this any longer. Write your plan here:

Aim to put what you have decided into action this week.

Myth Or Truth?

We all have to look after number one in life, because there's no such thing as a free lunch.

"Whoever wants to save their life will lose it, but whoever loses their life for me will save it."

Luke 9:24

"What counts in making a happy marriage is not so much how compatible you are, but how you deal with incompatibility."

Leo Tolstoy

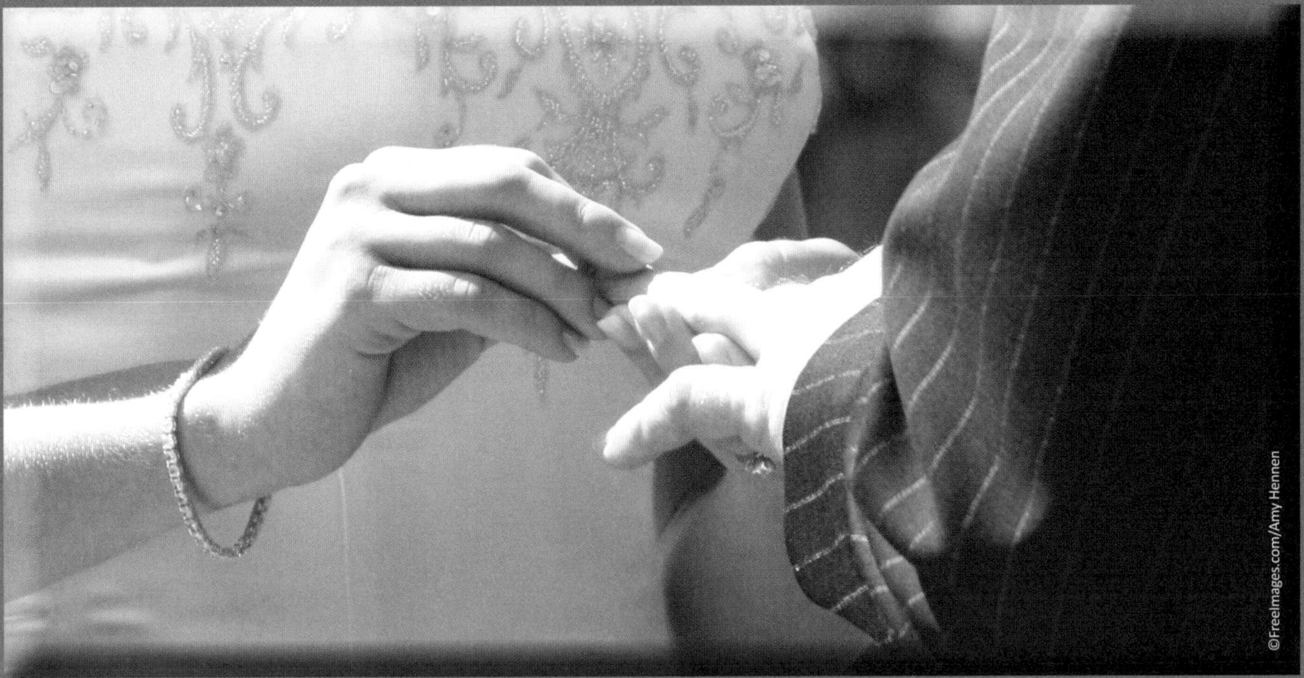

Differences & Diversity

Message

A dictionary definition of diversity is:

"To introduce variety or to redeem from uniformity or monotony."

Often couples are attracted to one another because of the ways in which they are different. Differences such as being either serious or fun loving, willing to take risks or having a more cautious nature appear to be complementary in the getting-to-know-you phase of a relationship. Our partner's character and personality traits can bring us life and lift us out of our own limitations. They can help us to be and do more than we would otherwise be capable of.

At first this is exciting!

However, as time goes by, and the busyness of life crowds in, we can find our differences creating more friction than harmony. The process of allowing our own character to be developed through another person's gifts and strengths is demanding of our time, energy and attention. It takes courage, humility and selflessness.

Thus, after some time, many couples conclude that they were not as compatible as they had first thought. Their diversity becomes a source of great irritation between them. Resistance to change results in them majoring on the negative aspects of their differences and can create high levels of disagreement.

The antidote for this irritation is to see the redemptive power our differences can offer us. Returning to the thought captured in the dictionary definition: diversity can redeem us from the monotony of being locked up by ourselves in the uniform smallness of our own world.

©iStockphoto.com/ PeopleImages

Meditation

"We each have natural inclinations in varying degrees from extroversion to introversion, as well as preference patterns for perceiving information, making decisions, and structuring our life and time. When we try to change our spouse's natural personality patterns, we negate his or her essential goodness and usually cause resentment, hurt and distrust."
Personality Differences by Judy Clark, Why Can't You Be More Like Me?

"The difficulty with marriage is that we fall in love with a personality, but must live with a character." Peter De Vries

©iStockphoto.com/&#169 Audrey Roorda

©iStockphoto.com/Mitchel Evans

©iStockphoto.com/Jan Tyler

D

Micro Story

"Pete is outgoing. He likes parties and initiates conversation by asking many open questions. I am more reserved and prefer to socialise with one friend at a time. I used to get hurt when Pete would leave me to fend for myself at a party. He didn't understand how uncomfortable it felt for me.

I am highly organised and pay close attention to details. I look after the budget and keep careful records of how we spend money. In our early years Pete felt restricted by this approach as he has an easy going nature, and wants to be generous when among friends. As a result, he used to let money slip through his fingers unnoticed, and this was a constant source of conflict between us.

Pete doesn't mind getting into a good argument; in fact he quite enjoys it. He likes to analyse situations and events and he can be very persuasive. He doesn't really notice people's feelings and is quite happy for conversations to get heated if necessary. It used to frustrate him when I would try to point out that he wasn't listening to me because he was far too busy trying to prove his point.

He is a stickler for punctuality and always insists we get to places on time. He prefers life on a schedule and would not think of being late himself. I have had to learn it is important for our relationship that I don't keep him waiting, but he has also had to admit that the world doesn't end if we are two minutes late getting out of the house!"

Gina (aged 37)

Mr and Mrs Smith tried re-inventing themselves many times, but eventually had to accept there were some differences between them that would never change.

Model

We often picture ourselves tied on to opposite ends of a bungee strap! When we find ourselves pulling in opposite directions, the cord gets under tension until we can't take any more pressure and we stop pulling away and snap back to the middle - which can be painful!

Early in our marriage we had some quite extreme differences, but gradually we are learning to appreciate each other, rather than trying to become like each other or to make the other person change.

When we looked at our differing personality traits, we began to see why we were in conflict.

This was how our profiles shaped up:

You can see how very different we are, and I'm sure you can imagine the difficulties we were prone to experiencing! We have come to understand that what can seem like a **weakness** in the other person can actually be a **strength**, when it's contributed to the relationship in the right way. We are now learning to create **harmony** through our differences rather than causing **friction**.

JOHN	SUE
Extrovert	Introvert
Flexible	Strong minded
Cautious	Risk taker
Finisher	Starter
Makes allowances	Perfectionist
Non-confrontational	Able to probe or confront
Logical	Emotional
Saver	Spender
Energy / drive	Calmness / patience
Quick to let go	Over sensitive / analytical
Humorous	Serious minded
Likes stability	Enjoys change
Concrete thinker	Lateral thinker
Executer / achiever	Planner / organiser

Personality Profiles

Use this extended list of positive personality traits to develop your understanding of yourself and the differences between you and your mate:

1. adventurous
2. affectionate
3. ambitious
4. brave
5. bubbly
6. candid
7. careful
8. caring
9. cautious
10. cheerful
11. confident
12. considerate
13. co-operative
14. courteous
15. curious
16. daring
17. decisive
18. determined
19. devoted
20. diligent
21. disciplined
22. enthusiastic
23. extrovert
24. faithful
25. flexible
26. focused
27. forgiving
28. friendly
29. frugal
30. fun-loving
31. generous
32. gracious
33. grateful
34. hard-working
35. honest
36. humble
37. independent
38. interested
39. introvert
40. involved
41. jolly
42. kind
43. loving
44. loyal
45. mature
46. motivated
47. open-minded
48. optimistic
49. organised
50. perfectionist
51. practical
52. punctual
53. persuasive
54. quiet
55. realistic
56. reflective
57. reliable
58. responsible
59. selfless
60. sensitive
61. serious
62. silly
63. sincere
64. sympathetic
65. talkative
66. thoughtful
67. thrifty
68. tolerant
69. trusting
70. willing

Add any more that come to mind.....

Myth Or Truth?

Men are from Mars and women are from Venus.

D

Every person on earth is unique and therefore every close relationship requires a great deal of adjustment by both parties.

Mission "Drains or Radiators"

WEEK 1: Your mission is to discuss your differences and to see how you can use them to bring your relationship to life.

Using the list of personality traits on page 22, build your own profile and ask your husband or wife to build theirs. Draw lines to connect any opposites.

ME	YOU

WEEK 2: Your mission is to move away from the damage of unhelpful comparisons and to be more able to enjoy your diversity.

Looking back at your personality profiles, think about any ways in which you have tended to compare yourself unfavourably with your husband or wife because of your differences.

One way in which I have compared myself to my husband or wife which has had an unhelpful effect is:

Talk to each other about how you can each be free of these comparisons.

Thinking back to your discussion last week, now write down the most important thing you could do to reduce friction and increase harmony between you:

Write your own definition of compatibility:

Ego & Equality

Message

The Oxford English Dictionary describes the ego as a person's own sense of self-esteem or self-importance. Our relationships will thrive or fail according to whether we are able to walk the narrow path between the wrong attitudes of either false humility or an over inflated view of ourselves. Some people parade an image of worthlessness, drawing attention to their failures and weaknesses, so that friends and family will feel obliged to meet their needs. Others trumpet their successes and strengths in order to attract the affirmation they desire.

Developing a healthy relationship with our own ego is a challenging process. The extent to which we succeed will be reflected in the closeness we experience in our relationships. CS Lewis explained the balance that can be achieved, when he wrote,

"Humility is not thinking less of yourself but thinking of yourself less."

With this attitude we can be realistically positive about ourselves, acknowledging our own strengths and talents but, by not desiring to be in the limelight, we are also able to allow others to flourish in our presence.

If we can keep the CS Lewis principle in mind and work towards it as a goal, we will have a healthy mindset regarding the type of equality we expect to experience in marriage. When applying the word "equality" to a relationship, different scenarios spring to mind. There can be no doubt that men and women possess different attributes, and that no two individuals have exactly the same features, personalities or skill sets. So, in what ways should we consider one another as equals? Is equality something to which we have a right? There are various quotations for you to consider in the meditation section this week, which will hopefully help you to answer these two questions from your own perspective.

Myth Or Truth?

"Look out for Number One. If you don't, no one else will."

Arnold Rothstein

"A man can counterfeit love, he can counterfeit faith, he can counterfeit hope and all the other graces, but it is very difficult to counterfeit humility."

D. L. Moody

Mission "The Selfie Snapshot"

WEEK 1: Your mission is to take stock of your ego. Either take a selfie snapshot and paste it into the space below, or draw a cartoon image of yourself. Now look at the statements alongside your picture and tick either the yes [Y], no [N] or maybe [M] boxes as you feel they best apply to you.

- [Y] [N] [M] 1. When people compliment me, I often point out something bad about myself in reply.
- [Y] [N] [M] 2. I am happy with who I am.
- [Y] [N] [M] 3. I find it hard to listen to others, they bore me.
- [Y] [N] [M] 4. I talk a lot about the things that interest me.
- [Y] [N] [M] 5. I have some ambitious goals and won't allow anyone to stand in my way.
- [Y] [N] [M] 6. I worry about what people think of me.
- [Y] [N] [M] 7. I am comfortable in my own skin.
- [Y] [N] [M] 8. Anything I try to do goes wrong.
- [Y] [N] [M] 9. I get on well with everyone.
- [Y] [N] [M] 10. I get edgy when people interrupt my schedule for the day.
- [Y] [N] [M] 11. I feel a failure most of the time.
- [Y] [N] [M] 12. I am content with my lot in life.
- [Y] [N] [M] 13. I make plans and I like to stick to them.
- [Y] [N] [M] 14. Nobody understands me.
- [Y] [N] [M] 15. I enjoy listening to people and empathising with their troubles.
- [Y] [N] [M] 16. I hate myself.
- [Y] [N] [M] 17. What I earn is more important to me than who my neighbours are.
- [Y] [N] [M] 18. I am good at what I do.
- [Y] [N] [M] 19. It's important to me to dress so that others will compliment my appearance.
- [Y] [N] [M] 20. People add interest and excitement to my life.
- [Y] [N] [M] 21. I am a social misfit and often make a fool of myself.

Ask your husband or wife if they think your judgment is correct. If you agree with any adjustments your spouse suggests you make, change your responses accordingly. Then turn to the Ego Quiz scores on page 27 to discover how well balanced your ego is.

WEEK 2: Your mission is to define the kind of equality necessary for a great marriage.
Look over all the quotations on page 27 and pick the one that you find the most meaningful. Write a couple of sentences saying how it could apply to your marriage:

Next decide whether you agree [A] or disagree [D] with the following ideas about equality.
Husbands and wives have (or should have) equal:

- [A] [D] 1. abilities
- [A] [D] 2. say in making decisions
- [A] [D] 3. freedom
- [A] [D] 4. responsibilities
- [A] [D] 5. roles

Share your answers and discuss your thoughts with each other.

"All animals are equal, but some animals are more equal than others."

George Orwell

Micro Story

"I have struggled for many years with the concept of loving myself. I could never work out the difference between loving myself and being selfish. I grew up knowing that I was supposed to love other people and it seemed to me that, in order to do this, I couldn't love myself. The constant dilemmas of daily life, choices such as whether to buy something for myself or give the money to charity, compounded year on year to make me feel worse, because I would mostly choose the selfish options and I knew very well how self-centred I was. So I had to squash the voice of my conscience in order not to love myself less and less.

Then I got married! Of course I loved my husband, but living in close relationship with another person only highlighted my predicament even more. The only way I knew of dealing with the guilt I felt about being so self centred and yet hating myself for it, was to point out all my faults to my husband, in the hope that he would tell me they weren't true, and that I would receive from him some of the affirmation and love I so desperately wanted. Of course it didn't work.

What has worked is to begin to realise how loved I am, in spite of my faults, and to accept myself for who I am. When I accept and receive the love that others offer, I can begin to learn how to be as kind and patient with myself as I want to be with them.

I have a long way to go, but I now believe it is possible to love others as I love myself. It can be both/and, rather than either/or. I love myself a lot more when I am being kind and patient and generous towards others and can now see the difference between loving myself and being selfish. The thing I most love about myself these days is when I catch myself being unselfish! So the more unselfish I am, the more I love myself. I'm now in a win/win situation instead of losing out to myself all the time!"

Sue

Scores for the Ego Quiz

For each question that you ticked the "yes" column award yourself the corresponding letter from this list:

1. W	8. W	15. C
2. C	9. C	16. W
3. A	10. A	17. A
4. A	11. W	18. C
5. A	12. C	19. A
6. W	13. A	20. C
7. C	14. W	21. W

©iStockphoto.com/ VladimirFLoyd

©iStockphoto.com/AND-ONE

Total your number of each letter here:
Total As =   Total Cs =   Total Ws =
The letter for which you have the highest total shows your tendency towards being:

A – arrogant
C – contented
W – worthless

Look back at which statements are the C statements and pick one for which you answered no or maybe. Make it your focus for the week to work towards this kind of attitude.

Meditation

Consider your reactions to each of these quotations:

"If you want to see the true measure of a man, watch how he treats his inferiors, not his equals." Sirius Black in Harry Potter and the Goblet of Fire, by J K Rowling

"The worst form of inequality is to try to make unequal things equal." Aristotle

"Humility is freedom from your own driven ego." Martha Kilpatrick

"A candle loses nothing of its light by lighting another candle." Father James Keller

"My one regret in life is that I am not someone else." Woody Allen

"Do not think of yourself more highly than you ought, but rather think of yourself with sober judgment….." Romans 12:3

"The meek man is not a human mouse afflicted with a sense of his own inferiority. Rather he may be in his moral life as bold as a lion and as strong as Samson; but he has stopped being fooled about himself. He has accepted God's estimate of his own life. He knows he is as weak and as helpless as God has declared him to be, but paradoxically, he knows at the same time that he is of more importance than angels: in himself, nothing: in God, everything. That is his motto. He knows well that the world will never see him as God sees him and he has stopped caring." A. W. Tozer, The Pursuit of God

©FreeImages.com/G Schouten de Jel

Flashpoints & Filters

Message

Every relationship is likely to have its own particular triggers that cause conflict. Although there are many ways in which we will be willing and able to change to accommodate one another as the years go by, some of our differences may never be reconcilable. If we don't learn to overcome our negative reactions to these irritations, they will eventually establish subconscious flashpoints which erode our intimacy. Rob Parsons, founder of Care for the Family, describes the effect that small unresolved hurts have on a marriage as a "creeping separateness". We can find ourselves either flaring up or sulking over insignificant issues because of a backlog of previous minor controversies that we have buried instead of talking them out and finding the strength to forgive.

Living with unforgiveness creates an atmosphere in which it is very difficult to believe the best about the other person. Instead we are inclined to pass blame and make judgments about each other all too easily. We want to fight our own corner and we find it hard to see the other person's point of view. In effect, our vision becomes clouded as if we are viewing situations through a coloured filter. This type of filtering of what we hear and see is a predisposition to a certain opinion which makes us biased and unable to grasp the real truth. There are five main springboards for filters which can be categorised under the following headings:

- Distractions
- Emotional states
- Beliefs and expectations
- Differences in style
- Self-protection

Filter Examples

Here are some practical examples of the kind of thoughts we might find ourselves having if we are filtering what our spouse is saying. You might like to decide as you read them which of the five categories they might fall into:

- We disagree and I'm convinced that my perspective is "right" and his/her view is "wrong".
- I'm not very interested in what he/she is talking about.
- I think I know what he/she is going to say, even before he/she starts speaking.
- I don't like the way he/she hints at things or his/her tone of voice.
- I get distracted from hearing what he/she is saying by other things going on around us.
- I feel too vulnerable to open myself up to his/her point of view.
- I don't think he/she cares about my feelings.
- He/she is always pessimistic and will automatically take the opposite stance when I make a suggestion.
- He/she talks too deeply and makes everything complicated.
- He/she isn't being fair.
- I always end up losing/giving in when we argue.
- I need to protect myself from getting hurt/being rejected again.

We can be completely unaware of the effect these filters have on us, until we take a step away from the issue and look again with fresh eyes. This week's story may help you to understand yourself better, as you transfer this couple's discoveries into your own situations.

Meditation

"The stupid neither forgive nor forget; the naive forgive and forget; the wise forgive but do not forget." Thomas Szasz

"Forgiveness is not an occasional act, it is a constant attitude." Martin Luther King Jr.

"*Marriage is one lifelong act of forgiveness.*" Mike Mason

"As I walked out the door toward the gate that would lead to my freedom, I knew if I didn't leave my bitterness and hatred behind, I'd still be in prison." Nelson Mandela

Myth Or Truth?

Attack is the best form of defence.

"A gentle answer turns away wrath, but a harsh word stirs up anger." Proverbs 15:1

Mission "Points of View"

WEEK 1: Your mission is to begin to overcome your flashpoints. Write down one thing about your spouse that irritates you when thinking of situations in your daily life.

Arrange a time with each other, when you will both be relaxed, with the specific purpose of taking it in turns to explain your feelings about your issue. Be willing to hear what your spouse has to say in response. If it would be helpful, use a timer to allow each other equal slots in which to talk and to listen.

Try to write a plan here for a resolution on which you both agree:

WEEK 2:: Your mission is to identify your own filters.
Think about the times when you are not seeing "eye to eye" with each other and try to work out whether you have a filter in place that is hampering your vision.

By thinking about issues that have been irritating you recently, it may be possible to identify what the filter is that is keeping you from seeing your spouse's point of view on the matter. If you recognise that you may be using any of the example filters given on page 28, or others you have become aware of yourself, write what you have identified in the coloured lenses and then make it your aim this week to remove the filters and see things differently.

©iStockphoto.com/Fotovika

Macro Story

David came to understand filters through his clash with Sarah over a friendship:

"I met Graham as a colleague when I changed my job and started working away from home. He and his wife Diane invited me to lodge with them, which was a great escape from the loneliness of hotel rooms. Gradually my wife, Sarah, got to know their family as well and we would spend the occasional weekend together. I always thought how well we seemed to get on, even though their children were quite a lot younger than ours. I did notice during these weekends though, that Sarah was sometimes quieter than her normal self and not always enthusiastic about my suggestions to plan further opportunities to spend time with them. I sensed she saw them as more my friends than hers. Even though I tried to include her as much as possible, she would tell me that she often felt left out when conversations centred around work or things I had talked about with Graham and Diane during my many evenings spent either playing sport with Graham, or having dinner and watching TV or playing games with the family.

I knew she was doing her best to hold the fort at home in my absence. She knew I would rather have worked closer to home if that had been possible. But, with circumstances as they were, in her eyes I was living half of each week with my "second family".

Our two families kept in touch with visits and weekends, even after my periods of working away had come to an end, until the time eventually came when Graham was offered a move abroad. By this time our children were independent enough for us to fly half way round the world without them. So we visited Graham and Diane three times during the next eight years, combining our visits with their family holiday plans to explore the country. We have never really been fans of the foreign culture, but enjoyed the experiences for what they were.

Last year, we were invited to go again and this time Sarah initially refused. She gave a number of reasons: finances, long journeys, language difficulties, not enjoying foreign food, culture differences and generally preferring to holiday in this country. But the only reason I really took on board was that she said she found it difficult to spend that amount of concentrated time with Graham and Diane. My initial reaction was to feel offended, on my own behalf as well as theirs. It seemed introverted to the point of being rude that she could possibly have trouble getting on with these people that I classed among our best friends.

We talked about it awkwardly. We both sulked for a while, mulling it over. My first reaction was to say I couldn't go without her and if we didn't go, the friendship with them would be over. Then I said I would go on my own. Then Sarah said she would come after all, for a short time and with certain other conditions attached. By then I felt it wasn't going to be a happy experience even if we did go

"You definitely grunt more lovingly these days, since we've been practising our communication skills!"

together. It seemed to me that Sarah was being difficult, just to make the point that it wasn't her first choice of either holiday or friends. We dropped the subject for a couple of months as there was no urgency to make a decision, but it became the "elephant in the room". At any slight mention of holiday plans in conversation with others, there was tension.

One day, in a book I was reading, I came across the concept of listening through filters. Applying what I had read to our situation, I began to see how the historical one-sidedness of our friendship with Graham and Diane (which was nobody's fault) had meant that I had allowed a filter to develop in the way I approached any conversation about them with Sarah. I had adopted a predisposition to believe that she was annoyed that I had a good friendship with them and that she didn't want to share in it. This filter coloured everything I heard her saying about her views on another visit to see them.

But it wasn't true. It wasn't the full picture. In fact she had tried really hard with the friendship, and enjoyed it, but now with the huge distance between us and over ten years since they had left England, things had changed. To spend a whole holiday together after not seeing or talking to one another for more than a brief Skype call now and then, with all of the other factors to consider as well, was daunting.

With this new understanding, I was able to take a more honest look at Sarah's entire range of reasons, including the fact that she had already done all the planning and arranging of the three previous trips and had happily come with me on those occasions. I began to be able to see her point of view and to agree that without the close friendship to consider, I too would view the cost, the travelling and the culture to be reasons to think twice. We haven't as yet decided if we will go or not, but at least we are now more able to discuss it as if we are on the same team again.”

David

Gadgets & Games

Message

Computers, smartphones and other technological advances have enormously assisted the work environment of our current generation. However, they have also rained upon us a huge range of distractions in the form of gadgets and games that are snatching away our adult lives and ruining our relationships, unless we are being incredibly vigilant. Broadly speaking work and leisure may be categorised as opposite approaches to life. Through work, a person makes their contribution to the world, whereas through our leisure pursuits we make withdrawals: like credits and debits in a bank account. Work is how we give and leisure is our way of taking.

Our journey towards adulthood is a process during which we need to learn the maturity that refines the balance between our giving and our taking.

When children grow up in times of war or other great hardship they often grow into responsibility more quickly than those who are brought up with all their needs and wants provided for. Everybody needs to be able to rest and there is nothing wrong with a little relaxation in our busy lives. However, we need to be masters of our leisure activities and not slaves to them. The same computer technology that has lightened our workload has also become the most dangerous hindrance to many people's productivity throughout the working day because of the distractions it can offer.

Of course screen time is not limited to our work lives. We now have more opportunities than ever before to indulge in an unending range of activities. We will do well to admit how addictive many of these activities can become.

Meditation

G

Read through the following list of different *"screen time"* activities and consider to what extent your relationship is affected (either positively or negatively) by each one. You may like to score each one on the minus 5 to plus 5 scale as appropriate.

-5 -4 -3 -2 -1 0 1 2 3 4 5 TV viewing
-5 -4 -3 -2 -1 0 1 2 3 4 5 I player
-5 -4 -3 -2 -1 0 1 2 3 4 5 You Tube
-5 -4 -3 -2 -1 0 1 2 3 4 5 Emailing
-5 -4 -3 -2 -1 0 1 2 3 4 5 Writing blogs
-5 -4 -3 -2 -1 0 1 2 3 4 5 On line shopping
-5 -4 -3 -2 -1 0 1 2 3 4 5 Surfing the internet – any particularly strong traits?
-5 -4 -3 -2 -1 0 1 2 3 4 5 On line gambling
-5 -4 -3 -2 -1 0 1 2 3 4 5 Pornography
-5 -4 -3 -2 -1 0 1 2 3 4 5 Social media sites
-5 -4 -3 -2 -1 0 1 2 3 4 5 Skype / Facetime calls
-5 -4 -3 -2 -1 0 1 2 3 4 5 Texting
-5 -4 -3 -2 -1 0 1 2 3 4 5 X Box / PlayStation etc
-5 -4 -3 -2 -1 0 1 2 3 4 5 Interactive gaming websites
-5 -4 -3 -2 -1 0 1 2 3 4 5 Graphic design
-5 -4 -3 -2 -1 0 1 2 3 4 5 Photo art
-5 -4 -3 -2 -1 0 1 2 3 4 5 Other applications

Mission "Turning Off and Tuning In"

WEEK 1: Use the chart below to assess your screen time (which falls into the category of leisure rather than work) over the course of the coming week. To get you started, the first few rows of the chart have been set up with options such as TV and phone, which we guess will be common to everyone. Subsequent rows have been left blank for you to enter other items from the list in the meditation section that apply to you, as not everybody will use the same combination of media. Be honest with yourself. Make sure you jot down every session, down to even the smallest incidences, so that you can then add up a total time per day:

	Mon	Tues	Wed	Thu	Fri	Sat	Sun
TV							
Email							
Texts							
Phone							
Total screen time per day							

WEEK 2: This week the challenge is to assess the impact of your screen time on your relationship. Look back on the charts you filled in for the past week and discuss the following questions:

- Are you addicted to any habits that create a negative impact on the relationship?
- Are any of your screen time hobbies overshadowing your togetherness?
- What are the main sources of conflict over screen time between you?

Now write here any changes you agree to make:

©iStockphoto.com/AndreyPopov

Micro Story

"Lately, I've been feeling convicted about how much time and attention I give social media in my life. I'm disheartened by how much my confidence and peace come from the amount of affirmation I get from responses to a photo or status update. Even more so, how much I compare my life to other people's online. The internet is a new battlefield full of bombs waiting to destroy lives, whether it be pornography, cyber-bullying, or emotional affairs. The internet is, as Ryan calls it, "the wild west."

As a friend and I were driving together, we got into a conversation about how social media breeds anxiety, especially in us ladies – wives, mums, or singles ready to mingle. She said something I will never forget, "It's funny because if you had the ability to look outside the frame of that friend's 'perfect life' Instagram post, we would probably see a mess of things." What's outside the frame? What's just to the left or to the right? In other words, their reality probably isn't far from our own reality. Social media allows us to show pieces of our lives – and only the ones we choose to show, which are often just the greatest pieces and moments. This is not a bad thing. However the trouble begins when we start perceiving these as reality and not simply as beautiful moments in time.

Too many times I stumble into envying something in a person's life, be it peace, financial wealth, cute clothes, a husband who intentionally thinks about cooking dinner or bringing home flowers... whatever it is, I somehow find myself comparing and coveting (which is a sin!). Choosing to fight against this, I recently removed the Facebook app from my phone as it was continually adding to my insecurities and stealing precious time with my sweet baby girl and amazing hubby. Constantly checking it, constantly scrolling through feeds, was making me crazy, giving me anxiety and making me feel discontented with my life, my family... my situation. It was stealing the joy of today's blessings."

Selena

Selena Frederick, www.fiercemarriage.com

Myth Or Truth?

The world is my oyster.

“If you find honey, eat just enough — too much of it, and you will vomit.” Proverbs 25:16

Photography: Sue Roseblade

“*It has become appallingly obvious that our technology has exceeded our humanity.*” Albert Einstein

“*Technology is the knack of so arranging the world that we don't have to experience it.*” Max Frisch

Home & Hospitality

Message

For the next two weeks our focus is going to be on how we build a home and how we use it. There is no doubt about it: choosing and then maintaining our homes can consume a great deal of time and energy. Anything that requires great chunks of our time and energy is a potential source of stress between us. Whether we are building, buying, renovating or just decorating and furnishing a house there are many decisions, both small and large, which have to be agreed between us. The amount of choice we have in the western world can make the process long and complicated and we need to find methods by which we can simplify our decision making so that it doesn't burn us out.

Our home will become the nest within which to love each other and build our family but we will probably also want to use it now and then to be hospitable to others. Deciding how open a home we want to establish is often not something that a couple will think to discuss. It just happens over the course of time as we invite people round, or they feel free to drop in at any time of day or night! How much people turn up uninvited will probably depend on how welcoming we are of such visits. Some people prefer a less open home, making definite dates and times with their guests. Talking to our spouse about how we feel about allowing others to share our home can help us to become more purposeful in relating to our extended family, our friends and our community and it can also build our own sense of togetherness.

Meditation

“The strength of a nation derives from the integrity of the home.” Confucius

Do we as a couple have similar or very different views on who we share our home with and how we go about doing that? How does this make me feel?

©FreeImages.com/Teodora Vlaicu

Mission "Too Many Cooks?"

WEEK 1: Your mission is to assess the effect on you of how you each share in looking after your home.

By Yourself:

Alongside each role or task we have listed, write the name of the person who you think is mainly responsible or write "shared" if you take equal responsibility in that area. Then give a score out of 10 for each item on your list, where 10 means that you are totally happy with how that role is fulfilled, and 1 means that you are not at all happy with the way the responsibility is delegated.

Role or Task	Me / You / Shared	Score out of 10	Role or Task	Me / You / Shared	Score out of 10
Rubbish & recycling			Choosing décor		
Car maintenance			Furniture arrangement		
Laundry			Tidiness		
Ironing			Gardening		
Food shopping			Renovation work / DIY		
Meal planning			Dealing with post / emails		
Cooking			Making appointments		
Cleaning			Decorating		
Planning holidays			Checking the budget		
Arranging social events			Arranging date nights		

Together:

Compare your answers and compliment each other on the areas in which you have given high scores, thanking one another for what you do well.

Now choose one area each for which you gave a low score and discuss ways in which your approach to this task could be improved.

©iStockphoto.com/monkeybusinessimages

©iStockphoto.com/PeopleImages

WEEK 2: Your mission is to reassess your hospitality.

Start by making your own list of all the people who come into your home from time to time.

Now discuss the following questions with your husband or wife:

1. Are you both happy with how "open" your home is?

2. In what ways do you feel your circle of family, friends and neighbours benefit from your hospitality?

3. What changes, if any, would you like to make to the way you use your home?

Life's too short to explain why he can't watch the football once the guests arrive.
I just hide the remote in the laundry basket.

Micro Story

"My issue in looking after our home has always been a streak of perfectionism when it comes to tidiness. I have realised in recent years that although John isn't an untidy person, it is unfair of me to expect him to panda to all my quirks and desires for precision.

I began wearing glasses at the age of forty. At first they were reading glasses and came with all the irritations associated with taking them on and off, leaving them behind when going out, or remembering to take them with me and then forgetting to bring them home again. So when, a few years later, I came to need varifocal lenses, although I didn't like having to wear glasses all the time, it was relief not to have to keep worrying about where they were.

It was a few years later that John gave up his struggle to read fine print. He would draw attention to his frustration with having to take reading glasses on and off, and I would think "just deal with it"! His solution to the problem of needing to have them on hand at a moment's notice was to have a cheap pair for every pocket and every room in the house. He would leave them unfolded, ready-to-wear, alongside their open case in various prominent places. I like tidiness and found this quite annoying. Sometimes I couldn't help myself folding their arms shut, putting them in the case, closing the case and maybe even putting the case into a drawer. If my secret hope was that John might one day follow suit and put them away himself, it never worked! It was one of those annoying things that I just had to accept and I had to learn not to let it colour my attitude or spoil the atmosphere between us. You can imagine my delight when he bought his first pair of varifocal lenses!"

Sue

Myth Or Truth?

"Home is the place we love best and grumble the most." Billy Sunday

"Love begins by taking care of the closest ones - the ones at home." Mother Teresa

"By wisdom a house is built, and through understanding it is established;
through knowledge its rooms are filled with rare and beautiful treasures." Proverbs 24:3-4

"*Remember, you married her, you didn't hire her!*" Dr Phil

Intimacy & Initiation

Message

Long lasting sexual intimacy within marriage is one of the by-products of becoming skilful communicators. Our predisposition could be to either see it as the central purpose of our marriage or alternatively to view it as just the icing on the cake. A difference of opinion may put us at odds with each other and lead to rejection and resentment, if we are not able to talk about how we feel. Even for those of us well practised in the art of sharing our feelings, sex can still be one of the hardest of subjects to discuss.

Melissa Risso, a licensed marriage and family therapist says, "Studies have shown that sexual communication is directly linked to sexual satisfaction." Just as we need to communicate over how to bring up the family, what purchases to make, or where we will take our holidays, so sex isn't any different. We have to communicate honestly but kindly in order to understand each other and grow in intimacy.

One of the major difficulties we face in achieving true intimacy is that our desire for sex can be misguided by lust: the instinct that wants to take what we feel we need. It is a learning process, and sometimes a very long one, to realise that lust has to be given up and replaced with love: the capacity to give what the other person needs. Only when we love generously and selflessly, with the intention of seeking our spouse's fulfilment above our own, do we discover that the greatest reward is more than just physical satisfaction. It is oneness of body, mind and spirit.

If our plan to initiate a sexual encounter is motivated by selfishness, then whatever we do, our attempts to arouse our husband or wife are not likely to be well received. We may buy flowers, wine and a special meal, or put on soft music and turn the lights down low, but if we are more motivated to get than to give, our efforts may well be in vain. True love is taking the time and effort to know our spouse so well that we have their best interests at the top of our agenda. They will be subconsciously reading between the lines and, however well we try to hide our motivations, they will be able to tell whether the invitation is for our own benefit or theirs.

This may sound like a hard message. Who can learn to be sufficiently "other-focussed" to achieve this kind of generous behaviour? Well, perhaps this is the very purpose of marriage: to challenge our selfish human nature, in order to help us to become the people we are meant to be. The relationships of those who learn the subtle difference between lust and love will mature into a beautiful place.

There is so much that could be said about the art of good love-making, but what matters most is not what we have written here, but what we enable you to say to each other. So whatever situation you are in at the moment, do take the missions for this topic as a fantastic opportunity to move towards deeper intimacy by initiating some honest conversations.

Myth Or Truth?

A woman needs love to feel sexy; a man needs sex to feel loved.

"He who loves his wife, loves himself." Ephesians 5:28

Mission "Body Language"

WEEK 1: Your mission is to open up honest communication about sex.

Recommended reading before you begin your discussion:
www.desiringgod.org/articles/when-the-sex-should-stop

1. What do you find difficult to talk about in respect of sex?
Here are some suggestions to get you started:

- Use of words is awkward.
- We feel differently about it.
- I don't feel understood.
- I get embarrassed.
- I don't want to make you feel hurt or rejected.

2. What role does sex play in our marriage?
3. What does sex mean to me / you / our marriage?
4. What are my / your sexual wants, needs, desires?
5. What does it look like to be sexually happy in our marriage?

WEEK 2: Your mission is to fine tune your understanding of the arousal process and to develop your skills.

Actions and attitudes which feel to me like lust:	Actions and attitudes which feel to me like love:

Talk about how you most like love-making to be initiated.

Plan a three month experiment to improve your love-making as a result of your discussion, using the following agreements:

1. We will empty non-essentials from our diaries for three months.
2. We will both look out for opportunities to initiate love-making that we think will work well for the other person.
3. We will only initiate after careful consideration of the other person's health and schedule.
4. Neither of us will deny the other's advances during this experiment so that the fear of rejection is eliminated.
5. We will only expect love-making to consist of what we are both comfortable doing.
6. We will put energy into general conversation and time together for having fun.
7. We will continue talking about our feelings regularly.

Plan a date in your diaries now for a review of how the experiment has gone in three months' time. We will review the experiment on:

“To discover how I’m wired simply press today’s button sequence!

No, sorry, Wednesdays don’t always have the same sequence!”

Micro Story

“When Debbie and I were busy bringing in the money and bringing up the family, there wasn’t a lot of time left over for us as a couple. Mornings were never begun at our own volition. They were always either kicked off by the youngest child needing a feed or a change or a cuddle, or by the alarm clock once the kids had learned to sleep in a bit longer. I often thought about sex through the day and in the evenings I would hope we could get the kids asleep and the chores done in time for an early night.

I knew how busy Debbie’s days were though: more hectic than my eight hours at the office computer. I knew how tired she was by nine o’clock in the evening. In the early years I went upstairs regularly with the hope that she would initiate love-making. I didn’t suggest it myself, as the rejection I would feel if my offer was refused seemed worse than the resentment I was carrying. Night after night we would collapse into bed side by side with no more than a quick goodnight kiss and I would turn over in self pity and nurse my hurt pride without ever telling Debbie how I felt. My silent resentment grew as the months turned into years. I blamed Debbie more and more, believing the ball was firmly in her court, because I knew I was willing and available, so the fact that sex wasn’t happening had to be all her fault.

Years on, and with the kids grown and flown, our relationship was hanging by a thread. We were both empty inside, and we knew we needed to talk. But we were each backed into our own corner and protecting the remnants of our fragile self esteem. Eventually, in the counsellor’s office, with the “D” word looming large over our heads, we began to unravel the knots we had tied ourselves in.”

Keith

Meditation

“Sex, whatever else it is, is an athletic skill. The more you practice, the more you can, the more you want to, the more you enjoy it, the less it tires you.”
Robert A. Heinlein, The Cat Who Walks Through Walls

“Sex does good things for our bodies, minds, emotions and our relationship. A marriage without sex has a couple of strikes against it, and less ability to deal with problems. I think what I see most is that regular sex can soften your feelings toward each other. It builds a sense of being a couple.”
Paul and Lori Byerly, The Marriage Bed

Dr. John M. Gottman, of The Gottman Institute in Seattle says: “It's all connected with really knowing one another, understanding one another and accepting one another and cherishing this person you love as irreplaceable.”

Spend a few minutes considering your instinctive reactions to this week's message and these quotes. Assess how you feel about your own sex life.

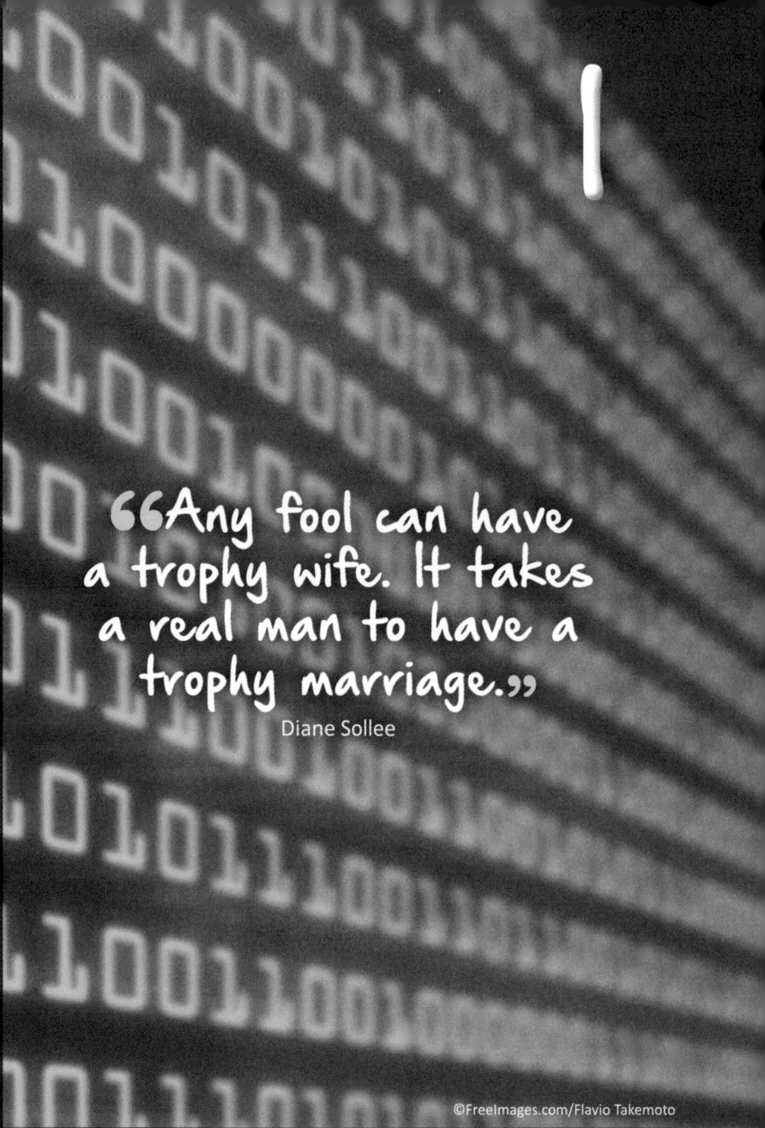

“Any fool can have a trophy wife. It takes a real man to have a trophy marriage.”
Diane Sollee

©FreeImages.com/Flavio Takemoto

©FreeImages.com/Jorc Navarro

Jibing & Jesting

Message

Humour is a wonderful asset in a marriage. It is a gift to possess the ability to make people laugh. However, we can easily be misguided in our thinking and end up using strategies which manipulate, undermine and control people, all under the guise of what we loosely term humour.

In a study by Rod A. Martin, reported in his book "The Psychology of Humor – an integrative approach", a questionnaire identified these four different types of humour:

- **Affiliative** – includes telling jokes or just saying funny things that are not at the expense of anybody. People use this type of humour to nurture relationships between themselves and others, to bring groups together, and create a more light-hearted and enjoyable atmosphere.

- **Self-defeating** – some people amuse others at their own expense. They'll make themselves the butt of their own jokes, and make fun of themselves to gain approval from others. They'll even laugh with everyone when others put them down.

- **Self-enhancing** – having the ability to find the funny in everyday situations, but it is mainly a way of coping with any adversity, and not letting negative emotions take over.

- **Aggressive** – includes teasing, making fun of others, some types of sarcasm, and putting others down. This type of humour is mostly hurtful, and can be used to manipulate and alienate others. People who use more aggressive humour can have trouble holding back from saying funny things.

Every person is going to use a little bit of each of these, and it's not necessarily a bad thing to use a little self-defeating or aggressive humour every now and then. For example, aggressive humour can be useful in confrontational situations, and wittiness can be shown off wrapped up in a bit of sarcasm. Self-defeating humour can be useful in proving you are not taking yourself too seriously, and will demonstrate to others that you can tolerate a little jabbing. In essence, it's good to have a mixture of these humour styles.
Excerpt taken from: "What Your Humor Style Can Reveal About Your Personality" by Jonathan Beber, MA

Interestingly the study showed that as we get older humour becomes less important to many people. The really important thing is to know what is appropriate for any given situation and audience. In a marriage, we should pay particular attention to how our humour is received, as it can be a powerful influence for either building or destroying closeness.

Meditation

"Be amusing: never tell unkind stories; above all, never tell long ones."
Benjamin Disraeli

"I've learned that people will forget what you said, people will forget what you did, but people will never forget how you made them feel."
Maya Angelou

"Make it dark, make it grim, make it tough, but then, for the love of God, tell a joke."
Joss Whedon

"Humour is what happens when we're told the truth quicker and more directly than we're used to."
George Saunders, The Braindead Megaphone

As a rule of thumb: laugh at yourself and laugh with your spouse.

Micro Story

"We got together in our late teens and one of the things I liked most about Marcus was his sense of humour. He was relaxed and light hearted and he balanced out the serious side of my nature really well. He was a clown who loved Monty Python and Fawlty Towers and a day would hardly go by without him finding several slick opportunities to quote from his favourite films or episodes. Any cutting remarks would be delivered with a dry wit that meant they bounced back on him, without causing pain. We did harmless but crazy things together, purely for the fun of it. We would wrestle each other on the floor and end up in a tangle of laughter and joy.

We look back now and wonder when it was we lost those people that we were. The quotes are still trotted out, but they have lost their sparkle. Little irritations give rise to more sarcasm than fun, and the pile of hurts that has amassed as a result have a cutting edge and a life of their own."

Kate (aged 55)

Mission "Only Joking"

WEEK 1: Your mission is to assess your own dominant humour style. Looking at the four types of humour on page 44, rate them in order of how much you think you tend to use them (where 1 is most and 4 is least):

1.
2.
3.
4.

Now consider them again and decide which order you would put them in according to how much you enjoy hearing others using them:

1.
2.
3.
4.

Thirdly order them again, specifically in relation to how you like your spouse to use them between the two of you:

1.
2.
3.
4.

Finally, discuss with each other how you feel about the types of humour you use both when you're alone together and also when in the company of others.

WEEK 2: Your mission is to consider a wider range of humour styles and how they could enhance your relationship: Read through the list of 20 different forms of humour on pages 46 & 47.

JIBING.....

Write in this box three forms of humour from the list of twenty that you think would be most damaging to your relationship and try to say why that would be.

JESTING.....

Now pick a selection of three that you think could work well between you. Write them here and give some thought as to the context in which you could use them. Write any notes or ideas that come to you, and plan to focus on looking for opportunities to try them out in the coming week.

Humour itself is merely the quality of something.....

While it depends largely on its intention, it also depends on how it is perceived by one's audience. Understanding the recipient's sense of humour is a major factor in terms of its degree of funniness. What humour does to others in terms of their health often varies. Good and appropriate humour can be life giving and inspirational, whilst inappropriate style or content can lower self esteem or breed resentment.

20 Types or Forms of Humour by Mark Nichol

Understand yourself by understanding the variety of comic expressions that people employ in different situations:

1. Anecdotal:

Named after the word anecdote (which stems from the Greek term meaning "unpublished"); refers to comic personal stories that may be true or partly true but embellished.

2. Blue:

Also called off-colour, or risqué (from the French word for "to risk"); relies on impropriety or indecency for comic effect. (The name probably derives from the eighteenth-century use of the word blue to refer to morally strict standards — hence the phrase "blue laws" to refer to ordinances restricting certain behaviour on the Sabbath).
A related type is broad humour, which refers to unrestrained, unsubtle humour often marked by coarse jokes and sexual situations.

3. Burlesque:

Ridicules by imitating with caricature, or exaggerated characterisation. The association with striptease is that in a bygone era, mocking skits and ecdysiast displays were often on the same playbills in certain venues.

4. Dark/Gallows/Morbid:

Grim or depressing humour dealing with misfortune and/or death and with a pessimistic outlook.

5. Deadpan/Dry:

Delivered with an impassive, expressionless, matter-of-fact presentation.

6. Droll:

From the Dutch word meaning "imp"; utilises capricious or eccentric humour.

7. Epigrammatic:

Humour consisting of a witty saying such as "Too many people run out of ideas long before they run out of words." (Not all epigrams are humorous, however.) Two masters of epigrammatic humour are Benjamin Franklin (as the author of Poor Richard's Almanack) and Oscar Wilde.

8. Farcical:

Comedy based on improbable coincidences and with satirical elements, punctuated at times with overwrought, frantic action. (It, like screwball comedy, shares many elements with a comedy of errors.) Movies and plays featuring the Marx Brothers are epitomes of farce. The adjective also refers to incidents or proceedings that seem too ridiculous to be true.

Myth Or Truth? . . . .

Sarcasm is the lowest form of wit.

“Life would be tragic if it weren’t funny.” Stephen Hawking

©iStockphoto.com/digitalskillet

9. High/Highbrow:

Humour pertaining to cultured, sophisticated themes.

10. Hyperbolic:

Comic presentation marked by extravagant exaggeration and outsized characterisation.

11. Ironic:

Humour involving incongruity and discordance with norms, in which the intended meaning is opposite, or nearly opposite, to the literal meaning. (Not all irony is humorous, however.)

12. Juvenile/Sophomoric:

Humour involving childish themes such as pranks, name-calling, and other immature behaviour.

13. Mordant:

Caustic or biting humour (the word stems from a Latin word meaning “to bite”). Not to be confused with morbid humour.

14. Parodic:

Imitation often intended to ridicule an author, an artistic endeavour, or a genre.

15. Satirical:

Humour that mocks human weaknesses or aspects of society.

16. Screwball:

Akin to farce in that it deals with unlikely situations and responses to those situations; distinguished, like farcical humour, by exaggerated characterisations and episodes of fast-paced action.

17. Self-deprecating:

Humour in which performers target themselves and their foibles or misfortunes for comic effect. Stand-up comedian Rodney Dangerfield was a practitioner of self-deprecating humour.

18. Situational:

Humour arising out of quotidian situations; it is the basis of sitcoms, or situation comedies. Situational comedies employ elements of farce, screwball, slapstick, and other types of humour.

19. Slapstick:

Comedy in which mock violence and simulated bodily harm are staged for comic effect; also called physical comedy. The name derives from a prop consisting of a stick with an attached piece of wood that slapped loudly against it when one comedian struck another with it, enhancing the effect. The Three Stooges were renowned for their slapstick comedy.

20. Stand-up:

A form of comedy delivery in which a comic entertains an audience with jokes and humorous stories. A stand-up comedian may employ one or more of the types of humour described here.

www.dailywritingtips.com

©FreeImages.com/Lotus Head

Knowledge & Kindness

Message

The Oxford Dictionary definition of knowledge is as follows: "Facts, information, and skills acquired through experience or education; the theoretical or practical understanding of a subject."

Our knowledge will grow and change throughout the whole course of our lives and it can serve us well in many different spheres of influence. It can be gained in a wide variety of ways. We may pursue it through a course of study or training, through reading, listening to or watching programmes, through asking questions, through observing processes or behaviours and so on.

However, the methods by which we learn are not as important as what we become as a result of our acquired knowledge. The Bible recognises this and puts a caveat on the usefulness of knowledge. 1 Corinthians 8:1 claims that knowledge puffs up while love builds up. The implication here is that the way in which we use our expertise and understanding will have a direct impact on those around us. At the two extremes of the continuum are selfishness and kindness. So the question we have to ask ourselves is whether we use our knowledge to good effect in our relationships, rather than as a tool for lording it over each other.

©FreeImages.com/Fabio Pusterla

©FreeImages.com/shho

K

Mission "Kiss and Tell"...

WEEK 1: Your mission is to identify the different sources from which you learn and to recognise what you gain from them.
We have listed a number of sources of learning and expected benefits below. They are just suggestions and you may like to think of extra ideas of your own.

Your task is to draw lines to match the SOURCES to their BENEFITS in the ways you feel are most true for you. So for example, perhaps you might go on an educational course in order to develop your career progression. You may end up with several lines either to or from the same words, as appropriate.

SOURCES	BENEFITS
Educational courses	healthy lifestyle
Training events	medical support
Private study	creative skills
TV / films	communication skills
Radio	wisdom
Internet	facts and information
Books	career progression
Newspapers	contentment
Magazines	general knowledge
Support groups	political understanding
Social media	acceptance of others
Friendships	awareness of international affairs
Family relationships	breadth of trivia
Work	people skills
Counselling	personal maturity
My own experiences / mistakes	assertiveness
Other people's experiences / mistakes	practical know-how
Clinics	disciplined lifestyle
My spouse	understanding myself
Church or other faith groups	local news

WEEK 2: Your mission is to develop greater skill in using your knowledge to feed your relationship.

Discuss with your spouse the ways in which you matched the lists of sources and benefits. Ask them to pick the matched pair from your list which they feel you use best to feed the relationship. Write in each other's magazines here:

You best feed our relationship through gaining knowledge from.....

Because you use it to.....

Now ask them to choose one source and benefit, which they feel has a negative impact on the relationship. Allow them to express how they would like you to change:

You could be kinder in the use of your knowledge of.....

It would help me if you.....

Use their suggestion as your focus for the week, aiming to be particularly kind to them in the ways they have suggested.

©Rgbstock.com/SisCiel

©Rgbstock.com/SisCiel

Myth Or Truth?

The best principle on which to build a relationship is:

a) "…..eye for eye and tooth for tooth." Matthew 5:38

b) "…..do to others as you would have them do to you." Luke 6:31

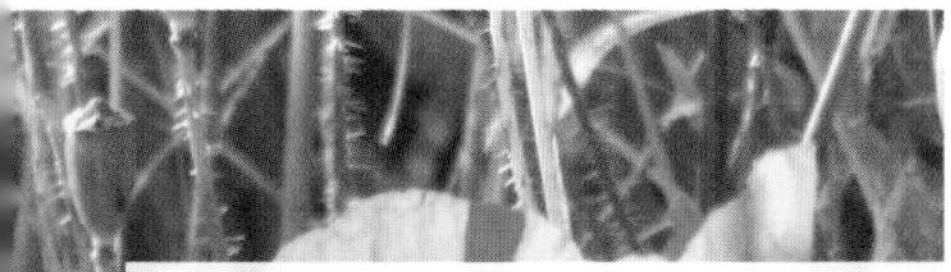

Meditation

"Kindness is the language which the deaf can hear and the blind can see." Mark Twain

"Carry out a random act of kindness, with no expectation of reward, safe in the knowledge that one day someone might do the same for you." Princess Diana

"Life is made up, not of great sacrifices or duties, but of little things, in which smiles and kindness, and small obligations given habitually, are what preserve the heart and secure comfort." Humphry Davy

"Ignorance is the curse of God; knowledge is the wing wherewith we fly to heaven." William Shakespeare

"Wisdom is the right use of knowledge. To know is not to be wise. Many men know a great deal, and are all the greater fools for it. There is no fool so great a fool as a knowing fool. But to know how to use knowledge is to have wisdom." Charles Spurgeon

Photography: Sue Roseblade

K

Micro Story

Giles (aged 32 and married 8 years) says:

"My wife, Lisa, is a teacher and her passion is for good spelling and grammar. She has been on courses as part of her training to become a Special Needs Coordinator and she's good at her job. The trouble is that spelling is not my strong point, but she loves to tell me about my mistakes. I used to ask her if I wasn't sure of how to spell a word, but she would go into long explanations of the rules and exceptions that applied, and I often felt she was scorning my inability to remember the knowledge she had imparted, when the same principle would come up on another occasion. These days I try to only send emails or write cards when she is out, so I know she won't be looking over my shoulder, and I use the spell check and a dictionary instead of asking for her help. I would love it if she could just tell me a correct spelling without that edge to her tone of voice that makes me feel small and stupid."

Giles

"Knowledge comes by taking things apart: analysis, but wisdom comes by putting things together."

John A Morrison

Leadership & Limitations

©FreeImages.com/Aleksandra P

Message

In marriage most of us have an innate sense that we are meant to experience an equal partnership. We believe in fairness. We expect help and encouragement, rather than opposition and control. Yet there are still many instances in which one or other of us wants to take charge or make an executive decision. Does the relationship need a leader, and if so, what should that look like in practice? Should a wife promise in her wedding vows to obey, or is that a faulty concept?

Perhaps the key to great leadership in a marriage is to be willing to understand and accept that the other person has limitations to their capabilities and their outlook on life, and that we too have our own set of limitations, which are just as frustrating to them. Marriages can be the source of a great deal of friction when we see our hopes and dreams thwarted by our spouse's apparent contrariness. Feelings of claustrophobia, being trapped or "tied down" are often expressed. These can surface as we have to continually bow to each other's wishes, consider each other's interests and adapt to each other's limitations and inconsistencies.

It is healthy to be able to see the limiting factors imposed on us by our becoming a couple, not as negative restrictions, but rather as guiding influences that help us pursue togetherness. If we ask ourselves not "What's good for me?" but instead, "What's good for us?" then we are leading by serving one another, and not many of us have any complaints about being served!

It may be that difficulties in decision making could be helped by considering the different facets of life for which you each take responsibility or have more expertise than your spouse. For example if you know more about cars than your spouse, perhaps you should have the final say when buying one. On the other hand, if you are looking for a mortgage or deciding where to invest some money, it may be your spouse who has more financial expertise and should therefore have the right to decide which bank or investment product to choose.

Myth Or Truth?

"Can two walk together, unless they are agreed?" Amos 3:3 NKJV

"How can you say to your brother (*or spouse*), 'Brother, let me take the speck out of your eye,' when you yourself fail to see the plank in your own eye? You hypocrite, first take the plank out of your eye, and then you will see clearly to remove the speck from your brother's eye." Luke 6:42 (italics added)

©FreeImages.com/Wong Mei Teng

L

Mission "Live to Serve"

WEEK 1: Your mission is to move towards a better understanding of your expectations of leadership in the marriage.

Write your answers to the following questions and then read each other's views and discuss your responses:

1. Does a marriage need one person to be allocated the role of leader for times when important decisions have to be made and the couple can't agree?

2. In which situations do you find yourself wanting to have the final say, but knowing that it won't be well received by your husband or wife?

3. What degree of independence and personal space to you think is healthy?

4. Which of the four attitudes to conflict in the table below would you say is your "go to" response (or does it vary according to the issue)? You have a total of 20 points to allocate to your own four response boxes in the "me" column. Share the points out, giving more points to attitudes that you are more likely to adopt, and less to those you rarely use, so that you can build up a picture of your behaviour. Then do the same with another 20 points and see if you can accurately rate your spouse's attitudes in the "you" column, before discussing your answers with each other.

	ME	YOU
I give in. I'd rather you had your way in order to keep the peace.		
I get out. I can't be doing with discussing the issue. Maybe it will just resolve itself if I ignore it.		
I win at all cost. Whatever the extent of the conflict it will be worth it to get what I want.		
I work towards the best solution for the relationship, even if it takes time, energy and some sacrifice on my part.		

Watch out for any conflict that arises this week and keep calm and quiet for long enough to consider which response you would normally have and which you will now choose to have.

WEEK 2: Your mission is to recognise and accept the limitations of being in relationship.

Asking the right questions is a GREAT way of finding out how to understand and accept each other!
Try discussing some of these questions:

1. What limitations does our marriage place on us as individuals?

2. What are our major shared purposes in life and are we heading in the right direction to achieve them?

3. Is there any aspect of our relationship that particularly makes you feel tied down or trapped?

4. What brings you the greatest feeling of satisfaction in life?

5. Having recognised the limitations of being a couple, how can we use what we do share to build togetherness?

Micro Story

Julia aged 47, divorced from Paul after 23 years of marriage, writes:

"I didn't promise to obey Paul when we got married. We both believed that it would be an equal partnership and that we would each take on the roles to which we were best suited. We thought we would make choices and decisions together and saw ourselves becoming a strong team. At first life was good. We talked through where we would go on holidays, how much we should spend on clothes or our social life, what kind of car would best meet our needs and so on. We had an eye for economy and were in agreement about how much we should save.

Seven years into the marriage our daughter arrived, followed just fifteen months later by our twin boys. The pressure the children put on our relationship was intense. We started to struggle financially as well as emotionally because we had no time or energy left for one another. Paul began doing more and more overtime, because it was obvious that I would not be able to go back to work at least until all three children were at school. Childcare would have cost more than I could earn. Fortunately my mother was on hand and was a great support during my long and otherwise lonely days. Subconsciously, I guess I began to depend on her for the emotional support that I was not getting from Paul.

We didn't really have time to stop and think about how we were drifting apart, but I do remember being aware of how much more dogmatic Paul was becoming as the children grew. He would come down heavily on one or other of them when he caught them in childish squabbles, without taking time to find out what had actually occurred. I would hear in no uncertain terms what he didn't want to do with his weekends, and suggestions I might make would be shot down in flames. In time he became quite detached from home and family life, preferring his own expensive leisure pursuits over spending time with me or the children. He no longer seemed to take any interest in deciding where we should go for a day out, or what we could do to decorate the house, and yet when I got on and made decisions without him, he never seemed approving. He would be quick to criticise the way I spent money on fun things for the kids, new curtains or some different colour paint for the living room walls.

I used to think that if only he could stop blaming me for the time, energy and money the children demanded of us, perhaps we could have talked more about finding the solutions we needed. Maybe if he had led the way in cutting back on his personal spending, we could have worked towards a budget for a family holiday or a weekend away for ourselves. If, just once in a while, he had taken the initiative to book us a babysitter, the relationship might have survived."

Julia

L

These are a few ways we can practise the humility of great leadership:

"To speak as little as possible of one's self.
To mind one's own business.
Not to want to manage other people's affairs.
To avoid curiosity.
To accept contradictions and correction cheerfully.
To pass over the mistakes of others.
To accept insults and injuries.
To accept being slighted, forgotten and disliked.
To be kind and gentle even under provocation.
Never to stand on one's dignity.
To choose always the hardest."

Mother Teresa, The Joy in Loving: A Guide to Daily Living

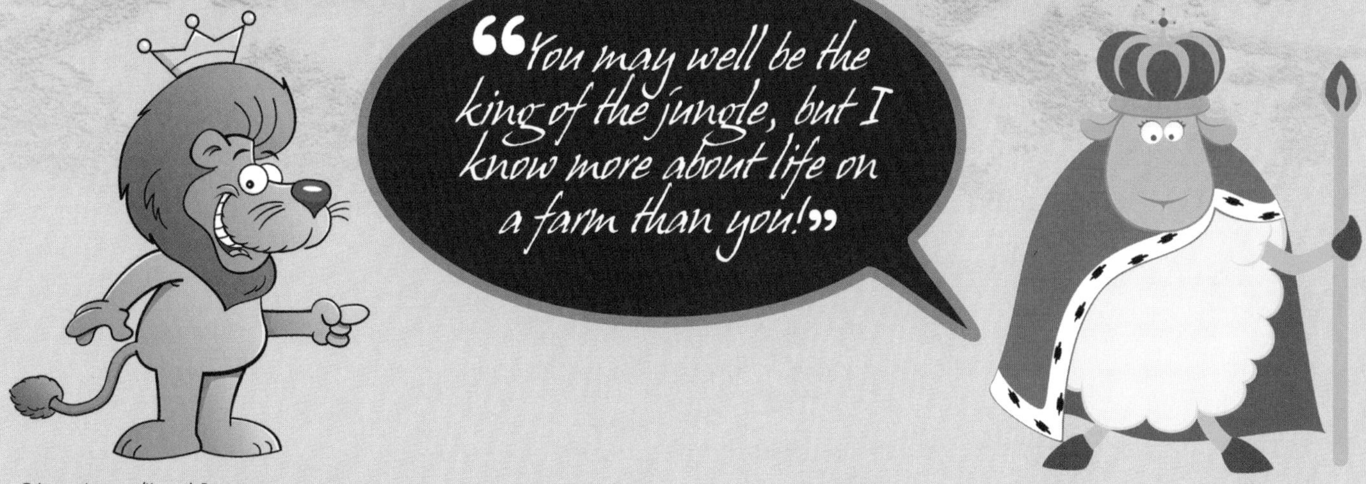

Meditation

Consider the following statements and decide the extent to which you agree or disagree with them. Circle your responses:

Leadership is a function not a status, a privilege and not a right.

Strongly Agree / Agree / Uncertain / Disagree / Strongly Disagree

Strong leadership is about being good at making decisions.

Strongly Agree / Agree / Uncertain / Disagree / Strongly Disagree

Neither of us has the right to demand submission to any course of action that is not good for the relationship, but both of us have the responsibility to only pursue pathways that will be good for the other and for the relationship itself.

Strongly Agree / Agree / Uncertain / Disagree / Strongly Disagree

Mystery & Mastery

©iStockphoto.com/andreusK

Message

©FreeImages.com/Keith Wilson

As human beings we are all mysterious to one another. We have been graced with the ability to think our own thoughts and to keep them private. It is only as we choose to share those thoughts with others that we form relationships. Many a relationship comes to ruin because the couple fail to understand one another.

Those failures partly happen as a result of poor communication skills, but also in lots of cases they are due to partners holding the preconception that people are complicated. I had my view on this subtly changed when I realised that a mystery could be described as being the KEY to something rather than the reason it's hidden from us. We are MEANT to find the answer to a mystery, to solve it like a riddle.

It is true that during the course of our growing up we do become complicated beings. Complications arise because of the damage that we suffer in our spirit as we are not perfectly loved and perfectly secure. We develop a whole range of protection mechanisms which act like a web of bondage around our hearts. We begin to wear a mask, or a variety of different masks, each appropriate for its own occasion, so that people will not cause us further injury, over and above the vulnerability that we already feel.

Wearing our masks causes us to make mistakes. We are uncertain as to which thoughts to keep private and which to divulge. We play cat and mouse games with people. We peep out from behind our masks in moments of great daring, only to retreat behind them again when the going gets tough. We love to comment on the mask another is wearing, whilst hoping that no one will notice or pass judgment on our own. Our complicated nature grows ever more mysterious as other people's damage bounces back onto us and compounds our insecurities. The marriage, which should be the security and love we need to be freed from our entanglement, turns out to only inflict more pain and devastation on our already crumbling self esteem. The web gets thicker and we are caught up in our own self-defeating attempts to escape. We promote and protect ourselves instead of reaching out in love to one another.

The good news is that mistakes can lead to maturity and messes to miracles if we learn how to help one another to escape from behind our masks. It may be that we are a mystery to ourselves as well as to our husband or wife. Some of our memories may have been so painful, that we have blotted them completely from our conscious minds. Until the pain from them is healed though, they will remain in our subconscious and contribute to the cords that keep us knotted up.

So how can we master the unravelling of this web of insecurity and mistrust? A long term relationship based on the commitment of the vows by which we promise to stick together through thick and thin gives us a great foundation, but we still need to learn how to turn the key to unlock the mysteries that hold us back. Maybe as you undertake your mission this week, you will take a step in that direction.

Mistakes can lead to maturity and messes to miracles!

M

Mission "Sign Language"

WEEK 1: Your mission is to recognise the signs of your developing maturity.

1. Think back to a mistake you remember making and write down how it made you feel and what you learned from it.

2. Write three ways in which you have seen your spouse mature or mellow in the last few years.

3. Is there something that you see in or know about your spouse, of which you think they are unaware?

4. What is it about your spouse that you find most confusing or complicated?

Share your answers.

WEEK 2: Your mission is to master the art of finding healing from a past hurt.

Choose a recent incident in which you felt hurt by or angry towards your husband or wife. Write your feelings here:

Consider carefully how you think they felt and what it might have been that caused them to respond towards you in the way they did. Write your understanding here:

Discuss sensitively whether there are issues from further back in their past that might have sparked their unhelpful response to you. Aim to understand their original pain.

Then swap roles and repeat the process with the issue they have raised.

Myth Or Truth?

“The greatest healing therapy is friendship and love.” Hubert H. Humphrey

“The true mystery of the world is the visible, not the invisible.” Oscar Wilde

“Mystery creates wonder, and wonder is the basis of man's desire to understand.” Neil Armstrong

“Transformation is my favourite game and, in my experience, anger and frustration are the result of you not being authentic somewhere in your life or with someone in your life. Being fake about anything creates a block inside of you. Life can't work for you if you don't show up as you.” Jason Mraz

“I suppose that since most of our hurts come through relationships so will our healing, and I know that grace rarely makes sense for those looking in from the outside.” Wm. Paul Young, The Shack

“You can run away from yourself so often, and so much, just because the broken pieces of you cut your feet too deeply if you stay around for too long. But then what if someone were to come along and pick up those pieces for you? Then you wouldn't have to run away from yourself anymore. You could stop running. If someone sees you as something worth staying with— maybe you'll stay with yourself, too.” C. JoyBell C

“It's important to make sure that we're talking with each other in a way that heals, not in a way that wounds.” Barack Obama

Meditation

“A woman’s heart should be so hidden in God that a man has to seek Him just to find her.” Maya Angelou

“The most intriguing people you will encounter in this life are the people who have insights about you, which you didn’t know about yourself.” Shannon L. Alder

How does it make you feel to think that your husband or wife might know things about you that you don’t know about yourself?

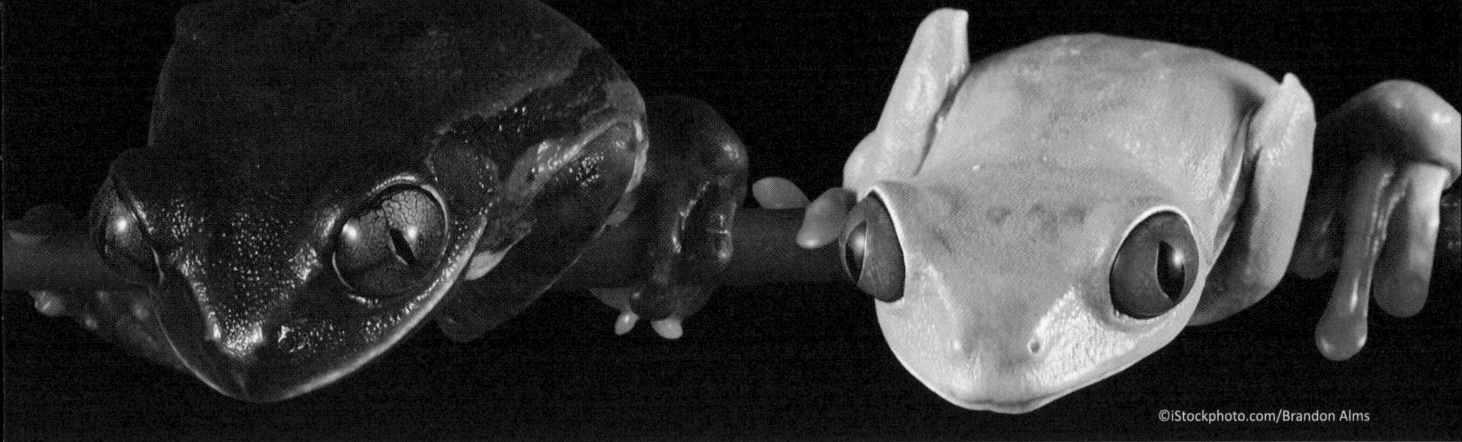

©iStockphoto.com/Brandon Alms

Macro Story

“I simply asked John who it was that had sent him a text. We had always told the family that we had no secrets from each other. Our emails and phones were shared territory, but on this occasion, he prickled.
“Why do you always have to pry?” he retorted.
“I was just interested.....” I tried to counter, remaining calm.
The silence that followed let me know that I wasn’t, on this occasion, going to get any further information, or an apology. I let the matter drop. I’m getting gradually better at doing that, although it still hurts every time.

About a week later, we were reading together on the sofa, when this time it was my phone that buzzed. An unkind thought popped into my mind and, as I read the text, I let it fester a few moments too long. Silently I read my message, and silently I picked up my book to continue reading.
“Who’s that?” he enquired, putting his finger in the page of his book, expecting a full and chatty explanation in reply.
“Why do you want to know?” I responded. As the words escaped my lips, I could see that his mind was pattern matching them with my question from the previous week, “I was just interested.....” His voice dropped as his sentence evaporated into the atmosphere, which, in that instant, had changed.

He prised the pages of his book apart; I prized my glorious revenge. Although I remembered from past experience that the temporary feeling of triumph would soon turn to ashes, yet again, I had used this self-defeating tactic.

We didn’t speak of the incident for a number of days, until we were together in the car, setting off for a weekend away. There had been a distance between us, tangible but buried. I knew my vengeful cloak of protection had turned to rags and my shame weighed on me like lead. Yet, the guilt was somehow dumbing down the pain of the hurt he had inflicted on me. He had started it. Was it really up to me to clear the air?

I broached the subject and, as expected, at first it didn’t go too well between us. We snapped and jibed at each other a few times, sparring for points as we emerged from our corners of defence.
I persevered with a gentle lead in line, “Can you think of any reason why you might have not felt like telling me about your text?”
“It wasn’t so much what you asked, but it was the tone of your voice. It felt like you were trying to control how I use my phone,” he replied.
We explored this thought for the best part of the next half hour and finally everything clicked into place. At a time a few years prior to this incident, when still on a pay-as-you-go tariff, he had been in a bit of a habit of sending texts back and forth with his brother, taking any number of messages to finalise an arrangement. I had found this frustrating as a call from the landline would have been free, and so I had dropped a number of hints to that effect, and had shown disapproval as the texts continued to fly. That period had been short lived and the problem had long since been overcome with a new phone and a new deal, but the wound of my controlling behaviour remained.

In our conversation that day I found the key to the mystery of his behaviour and the responsibility had been mine all along. Once we understood the root of where the outburst had come from, we were able to forgive each other. The wound is now just a scar which no longer pains him and we are able to use our little episode as a story to encourage others that life’s hurts can be healed.”

Sue

©FreeImages.com/Luca Baroncini

Noise & Nearness

Message

We all like to begin our day a certain way. French footwear designer, Christian Louboutin knows what he prefers. Describing his ideal wake up, he says: “Breakfast is a peaceful moment for me, so I never have the radio on, no music, no noise around. The only noise that is permitted is people’s voices. It’s a way for me to wake up without too much of a high speed feeling.”

Whether we identify with Christian, or prefer to start our day with a favourite DJ or TV presenter, we will probably have developed set patterns of behaviour in our morning routine. At other times of day, there will be those of us who like music or radio around the house and also in the car, and there will be those of us who don’t. In some homes the TV is on as background noise, while in others it is only turned on for specific programmes. When we live in close proximity to another human being, our background noise becomes theirs as well. Much of our personal space becomes shared with theirs, especially if our home is small and living space is limited.

For couples who each enjoy a very different atmosphere, this can be a great source of conflict. Often during their busy working years couples will manage their partner’s preferences quite well, but then be dismayed at how difficult it is to live with each other in retirement, when they are around each other so much more of the time. Alternatively, if one is busy and the other has very little to do, tension can rise as one gets under the other’s feet. One may be excellent at multi-tasking, whereas the other perhaps cannot think to write an email with someone looking over their shoulder, or even in the same room!

A conversation which acknowledges our various different styles and preferences will foster feelings of acceptance, and that in turn will help us work towards accommodating each other’s needs and preferences. As we talk, we will build closeness and dispel the tension that makes the relationship feel claustrophobic.

N

Meditation

1. What type and amount of noise do you enjoy and what do you dislike?

2. How well do you and your spouse manage your need for personal space?

"All of humanity's problems stem from man's inability to sit quietly in a room alone." Blaise Pascal, Pensées

Try sitting alone quietly for 10 minutes and feeling at peace. Aim to recognise anything that threatens to disturb that peace.

Micro Story

"I have had to learn that some things will never change. I can't expect us to enjoy the same things. We are different in lots of ways, but especially when it comes to music. Katie used to have certain types of music that she listened to, but once we had the family, I think her days were busy and noisy enough and her brain was juggling too many thoughts to have unnecessary noise crowding in on her. So she just never bothered with the radio or putting music on. I enjoy listening though, and in my view some types of music should be turned up loud. I know this aggravates Katie, so I try to be sensitive to that. I don't put music on as often as I'd like to, and I only turn it up really loud if she is out. I try to choose playlists that she won't mind too much if we're both around the house together.

It's all about knowing what works for her

Katie is a writer, and currently I am working from home as well. So if she is at the computer, I make sure she has the door shut, and I don't keep going in and out of the office, because I understand that she can't put sentences together if song lyrics are ringing through her head or if I keep interrupting her train of thought by talking to her. It's all about knowing what works for her and taking responsibility for making the relationship happy."

Bjorn (aged 45)

Mission "Up Close and Personal"

WEEK 1: Your mission is to appreciate the impact of noise on your relationship.

Rate each of the listed sources of noise as to how negatively or positively they affect you (where -5 is most negative and +5 is most positive) and then describe your feelings, giving reasons for the rating you have allocated. Add any other sources you wish in the spare rows:

Source of noise:	Rating:	Feelings:
Radio		
TV		
Music		
Snoring		
Chat		
Neighbours		
Traffic		
Game playing		
Equipment / Appliances		
Personal Habits		

Now discuss your charts with each other and look for possible solutions to any negative results.

WEEK 2: Your mission is to become more aware of each other's need for personal space.

Answer the following questions and then discuss your responses with each other:

1. Are there any particular times or scenarios when you feel the relationship is claustrophobic?

2. Is there enough physical space in your home for you to work with/around each other?
Are there any changes you could make?

3. Are there times when you don't have the solitude you feel you need for certain tasks?

Myth Or Truth?

N

Do you agree or disagree with the following observations?

"He who establishes his argument by noise and command shows that his reason is weak."
Michel de Montaigne

"One person's roar is another's whine, just as one person's music is another's unendurable noise."
Henry Rollins

"He who sleeps in continual noise is wakened by silence."
William Dean Howells, Silence is golden!

©FreeImages.com/Charlie Balch

Overload & Oneness

Photography: Sue Roseblade

Message

Each of us has the same twenty four hours in our day. For some of us it flies by; for others it drags. Technological advances have taken the strain from us in some areas of modern living, but they have added a variety of even more time-consuming activities instead. Perhaps we no longer spend a whole morning every week washing our clothes by hand and wringing them out with a mangle. Most of us these days don't even wash our dishes by hand, but are we more relaxed as a result? How do we use the time we save? Before we had our computers and our smart phones we had no need to check our emails every hour, or to see our old school friends' latest photos on Facebook the instant they appeared.

For some, the level of overload in their lives may be inescapable due to the stress of a demanding role at work. Alternatively, the pressure can be of our own making, perhaps caused by the dreams we are chasing. Either way, we can feel trapped by the sense that we have no control over the daily demands that not only snatch away our rest, but which also conspire to eat away at the heart of our relationships.

When we are busy, tired, stressed out or preoccupied we aren't able to love our husband or wife generously and unconditionally. We can end up short-changing one another and the delicate balance of giving and receiving can be subtly undermined. Oneness, which is the close feeling of togetherness we experience when all is right between us, plays fast and loose, and the blame game shows up centre stage.

Myth Or Truth?

Early to bed and early to rise, makes a man healthy, wealthy and wise.

A change is as good as a rest.

Meditation

Consider this claim: **"Commitment and availability are mutually exclusive."** Do you agree or disagree?

Commitments can be a good thing. They prove us responsible and reliable. They let other people know where they stand and what they can expect of us. They add integrity to our lives and people show us respect because of them. However, availability is only possible when we have sufficient slack in our schedule to juggle our time so that we can be flexible in response to important, urgent and incidental happenings as they occur. Otherwise interruptions to our routine can cause us to panic and react to the situation with an irritable attitude. Those of us who over-commit are probably the ones who struggle most with this irritation.

What things are you committed to and for what instances or people do you need to maintain availability?

How do your commitments affect your availability, either in a positive or a negative way?

Mission "Download – Upload"... O

WEEK 1: Your mission is to understand the elements of your life that create the feeling of overload. Sort the words and phrases in this list according to the categories of filling, neutral or draining below:

Walking in the countryside / tidiness / cleaning the house / a 10k run / being outdoors / a deep sleep / long journeys / being with happy people / time alone / spending money / cooking / a night out / driving / bringing work home / a day at home / listening to someone's troubles / an afternoon nap / answering emails / DIY tasks / doing my day job / a TV show / arguments / helping someone in need / being interrupted by a phone call / arranging a holiday / reading / golf / learning a new skill / ironing clothes / going out for a drink / cleaning the car / gardening / a take away dinner / family relationships / extreme sports / prayer / social media / dressing smartly / a day out / surfing the internet / playing a game / an unexpected visitor.

Add any of your own ideas into the mix as well.

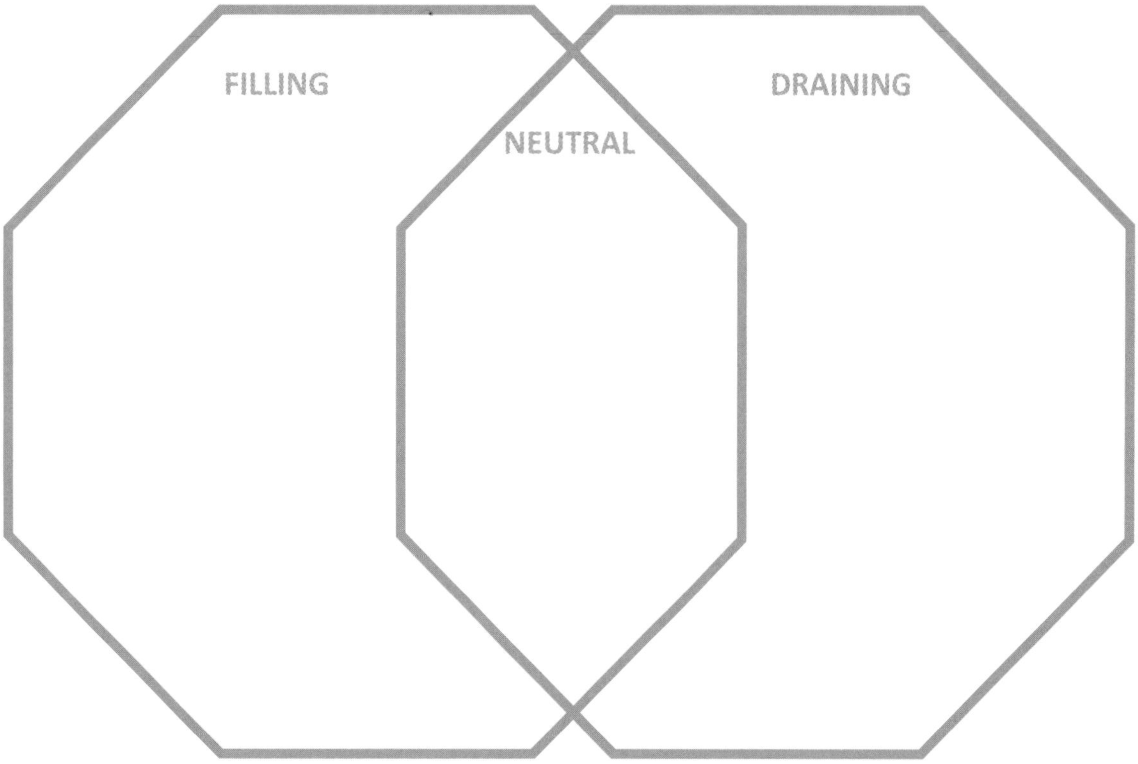

Underline one thing you wrote that you'd like to do more of and think about how you could make time for it this week.

Discuss the viability of the idea with your husband or wife.

Circle one thing you wrote that stresses you, which you would like to do something about.

Discuss with your husband or wife how you could instigate a change in this context.

WEEK 2: Your mission is to increase the level of oneness between you.
Remembering the change that your husband or wife wanted to instigate last week, plan how you could support them towards making the changes they desire. Write here what you plan to do:

Pay attention to any thoughts about how you might need to adapt in order to allow the changes to happen.
If last week's change was straightforward and has already come to fruition, ask your husband or wife to pick something else from their list and work on supporting them in this second context:

Be aware of improvements in your closeness in the week ahead as you play this interactive role that you have just described. Note here any differences your support is making to your oneness:

Macro Story

Hayden: “The idea of oneness fascinated me from the first time I heard the term. Interestingly there's only one letter different between the words openness and oneness. To achieve oneness we have had to learn how to maintain an openness at every opportunity, rather than letting little grudges and grievances cause us to shut down.

Somehow I knew this concept was what I had been wanting during the whole history of our marriage, but it had always seemed so elusive. Every now and then we would catch a glimpse of it on a day when we had set aside all the cares of life to focus on simply being together, but as soon as we returned to the demands of daily living it seemed to slip through our fingers again at the first cross word or the slightest misunderstanding.

I have discovered that oneness isn't something that I can pretend I have. I can't fake it, or work on it, or choose it on days I feel like having it. I have learned through painful experience that oneness is not a demand I can make of Stella, rather it's a reward that comes as I gradually learn the art of consistent selfless love. For us, oneness shows up when we have been particularly thoughtful and caring towards one another, quite often if we're on holiday or at least away from our usual levels of stress and busyness. At other times our attitudes have to be squeezed, not only through the confusing mincing machine of our gender and personality differences, but also that of our separate agendas, which can mean that, even if unintentionally, we hurt each other or make each other angry on a fairly regular basis. Add to that the baggage we brought into the relationship of our past hurts and you can easily begin to see why we haven't been able to live on this desired higher plane of existence for any length of time!

That's not to say that we don't enjoy some peace and harmony. We're not constantly fighting or even unhappy, but we know there's more to be enjoyed that we just can't seem to achieve. I'm sure sex is designed to bring us together but, although it adds to our closeness when we're already in a good place, it's not a magic wand. Stella tells me that for her sex starts in her thinking. So my challenge is to love the way her mind works! I have to learn how to be truly present with her and engage in her thought processes and concerns. As the male “hunter” I have learned that she needs to feel desired and cherished, otherwise she feels groped when I touch her. It's the quality of every little daily interaction that all adds to, or detracts from, her sense of how much I love her. One thoughtless comment, one over-reaction, one insensitive lack of awareness can mean that she will raise her barriers of self-protection. Then the vulnerability she needs to offer me in order for us to be ‘one', will be a long while returning. She struggles to open up to me in case I crush her again. It takes time to rebuild her trust and her confidence in being willing to be vulnerable.”

Hayden

©FreeImages.com/Mattox

Photography: Sue Roseblade

Stella: "In the early years of our marriage the pattern of events surrounding our sex life used to go a bit like this:

- We were busy and didn't get much past the kind of "download about the day" conversations.

- We had a few disagreements from time to time.

- A number of days would go by.

- Hayden would make hints implying we'd not had sex for a while, and I would take it as a dig that I was less keen than he was.

- That put me on the back foot – as if I was playing catch up in a game I could never win.

- I'd get the impression he thought it was my responsibility to initiate, because he didn't like the feeling of rejection if I wasn't immediately enthusiastic.

- I wished he would initiate with some loving attention and thoughtful words that would make me feel one with him, rather than either his almost too subtle hints or his outright requests.

- We'd make love, but I'd find it hard to get aroused because I didn't feel we were "one" with each other.

- Afterwards, he'd tell me how much he loved me. I'd wish he could have said all those nice things beforehand. I blamed him for not being more romantic towards me, which would have made me feel more wanted.

- We'd both end up feeling resentful that the other person hadn't fully met our needs.

Recently, however, I have at last begun to recognise that I have been far too quick to see it as all Hayden's fault that we didn't experience oneness more of the time. What I have understood is that I have the power to change my focus, by not blaming him for what he doesn't do or say in the lead up to making love. I am now much more careful to think about the good times we've had together and to do everything I possibly can to connect in positive ways at every level. I remind myself of the fact that when he wants to make love it isn't just for his own gratification, it's because he wants to give me pleasure. It's so easy to lose the idea that he's doing it for me as well as for himself, if I'm harbouring any resentment or feelings of rejection. If that's the case, I just feel used.

The times I feel most at one with Hayden are when we are on the same page physically, emotionally and spiritually. Sex can give us connection on all those levels but none of it happens automatically. If we just go about it as a purely physical act, then that's all we get from it.

I think Hayden has always wanted the emotional and spiritual connection just as much as I have, but I have had to help him to realise how these possible connections start to work through being able to communicate about our feelings. It has also helped to talk about agreeing the values we hold, sharing our goals and dreams and working towards them together. Often it has been when we've been in our worst moments of crisis, when we have had to really turn to each other for comfort, support and courage that our sex life has brought us the most oneness of all. I think, when we've been really up against it in life, our need for each other has outweighed our differences and that has drawn us close. Suddenly the small things that would upset us, don't loom so large in the light of a huge crisis. So it's been during those really difficult times that we have had the best and longest lasting sense of being one."

Stella

©FreeImages.com/DGBurns

"No, I haven't got time to go out for a drink.... I'm still searching for the perfect holiday!"

©iStockphoto.com/caracterdesign

Priorities & People

Micro Story

Maggi was a mum to four young children. Ten years into her marriage, she befriended Ellen, a mum of three, whom she had met at the toddler group she attended. She was good at listening and Ellen poured out her story in large chunks while the children played together. Ellen was separated from her husband who was now working abroad and had no contact with the family at all. Gradually the two mums spent more and more time together. Maggi was generally the hostess, as Ellen's rented flat was small and depressing and she liked being at Maggi's house, where the children had more space and a great supply of different toys.

Sometimes she was still there when Maggi's husband, Tom, came home from work. He was a generous natured guy and good with the kids. So it became common that they would stay for meals and sometimes even for the occasional sleepover, when the children pleaded to be allowed. Ellen would stay as well, as she didn't like going home to an empty flat. In the summer they would go out for picnics as an extended family, and although Tom and Maggi found it somewhat intrusive on their own time and space, they felt they were doing a great job in supporting Ellen's family unit.

One day Ellen happened to spot a holiday brochure on Maggi's coffee table, and somehow the conversation was drawn to the subject of how it would be fun to go away together. Maggi was unsure how she had landed herself in this awkward situation, and was beginning to feel vaguely uncomfortable with the turn the relationship was taking. The care that she felt for Ellen and the warmth of her friend's enthusiasm for the idea made it impossible for her to say no outright. The plan was left hanging and Maggi reported the conversation to Tom that evening. He wasn't against the idea per se, but as making holiday arrangements was definitely Maggi's forte rather than his, he left the ball very much in her court.

Later that week, at the travel agent's desk, as they waited for the assistant to be connected to the hotel receptionist, Ellen made a passing comment:

"It's great for Leah, Sam and Jason having Tom as their role model. They really need a father figure in their lives."

Maggi looked her friend in the eye and suddenly her own eyes were opened. She panicked on behalf of her family and from the momentary soul connection that comes with full on eye contact, she saw that she should also be concerned for her marriage. Tom had been too innocent to see it coming, but Maggi's mind now chased back through the past year and the many fleeting incidents between Ellen and Tom that her selfless nature had refused to acknowledge until now.

She hurriedly made the excuse that she had forgotten a dentist appointment, leaving behind the shop, her plans and her friendship in a blur of teary rage.

Message

Are people a blessing or an interruption in your day? Realistically, it will depend on who they are. Following on from your discussions on the subject of "overload" (if you are working through THE MAGAZINE in order) the idea of what fills or drains our energy reserves can be extended to different categories of people. Some people are like radiators: warming us up and giving us energy and life. Other people can be more like drains: in effect sucking the life out of us! It is important to have time for both.

How we fit people into our married life will very much depend on how differently we each enjoy being with others. One of you may have great patience for difficult people, being a good listener or of great practical support to needy individuals. Your husband or wife, may be the life and soul of any party, whereas you, on the other hand, may prefer to enjoy one-to-one time with friends or are happier in very small groups (or vice versa).

Myth Or Truth?

With which of the following well known sayings do you agree?

- Absence makes the heart grow fonder
- Out of sight out of mind
- Familiarity breeds contempt
- Good fences make good neighbours

"Welcome! I see you've brought the family..... No, my husband won't mind. We have nothing on tonight!"

©FreeImages.com/Yamamoto Ortiz

Meditation

"A perverse person stirs up conflict, and a gossip separates close friends." Proverbs 16:28

Are there any ways in which it would benefit your marriage if you were more cautious in your friendships?

Mission "Going Round in Circles"

WEEK 1: Your mission is to work out a priority schedule for your relationships.

It has been said that a couple need to spend at least 15 hours a week together (apart from time spent asleep)! This may or may not be realistic for you. Think through your routine and add up all the different slots of time that you are in each other's company. Write this figure in the first column of the chart, and then write in the second column what your desired amount of time would be.

Following on down the chart, enter your next most significant relationship in the second row and assess its current and desired time commitment in the same way. This may be a child, a parent, a close friend or other family member. Continue to add names in order of their priority in your life, allocating time allowances as you go. As you get further down your list of names, you may be entering monthly or bimonthly catch ups, or perhaps an even less regular allowance for people you are less close to.

You may find that some relationships are at present given more than the time that would be desirable and others less. Choose the person where the difference between the two figures is greatest and consider the reasons for the discrepancy.

Priority order:	Name	Current time	Desired time	Priority order:	Name	Current time	Desired time
1				11			
2				12			
3				13			
4				14			
5				15			
6				16			
7				17			
8				18			
9				19			
10				20			

Share your charts with each other and look for similarities in the time discrepancies of any names that you have both included. Discuss how you each feel about the time your spouse spends with other people. Then talk about the desired times you have written down for each other.

See if you can agree a comfortable ideal and talk about how you could work towards it.

WEEK 2: Your mission is to understand the effect other people have on your relationship and to make your contact with them work in favour of it, rather than in opposition to it.

Using the people on your chart from last week, and including others you may think of, write their names in the appropriate circles below (or across the borders if they don't always belong in the same category):

Large = needs support
Medium = brings a measure of life and enjoyment
Small = completely at ease with

Discuss together whether you think you are wise, sensible, cautious, innocent, thoughtful etc in these relationships and whether you have a good balance between the easier relationships and the more demanding or difficult ones. If the balance needs adjusting, talk about how you could work towards this and write down what needs to happen:

Make a plan here for your next social event and put the date in your diaries:

©FreeImages.com/Roy White

Quarrels & Quirkiness

Photography: Sue Roseblade

Message

Everyone will probably quarrel from time to time, but not everyone is quarrelsome by nature. Everyone has a few quirks; we wouldn't be normal without them. But not everyone is quirky to the point of being eccentric. So what is it that makes some of us quarrelsome and quirky and how can we save ourselves and each other from the traps they create?

The secret of putting forward your case without being quarrelsome is to develop a less pessimistic outlook on life. It is possible to disagree without being disagreeable. It is feasible to question someone's decision without being dogmatic. The challenge in avoiding extremes of eccentricity, as with most behaviour, is self awareness. It is part of your unique nature as a human being to be different from everyone else on the planet, but you can avoid extremes. You can learn to be more aware of the extent to which your personal mannerisms and habits are impinging on other people's enjoyment of your company and you can choose to adjust accordingly.

Having analysed our observations of other people over the past two weeks, maybe it is time to turn the tables and point the finger back at ourselves. Before looking at this week's meditation, have a quick flick back to last week's message to understand what we mean by radiators and drains.

Meditation

Ask yourself:

Am I the kind of person others see as being a *"radiator"* or a *"drain"*?

Think back through the names on your circles of contact in last week's mission and consider where you would fit in their circles.

Myth Or Truth?

"Criticism and pessimism destroy families, undermine institutions of all kinds, defeat nearly everyone, and spread a shroud of gloom over entire nations."

Gordon B. Hinckley

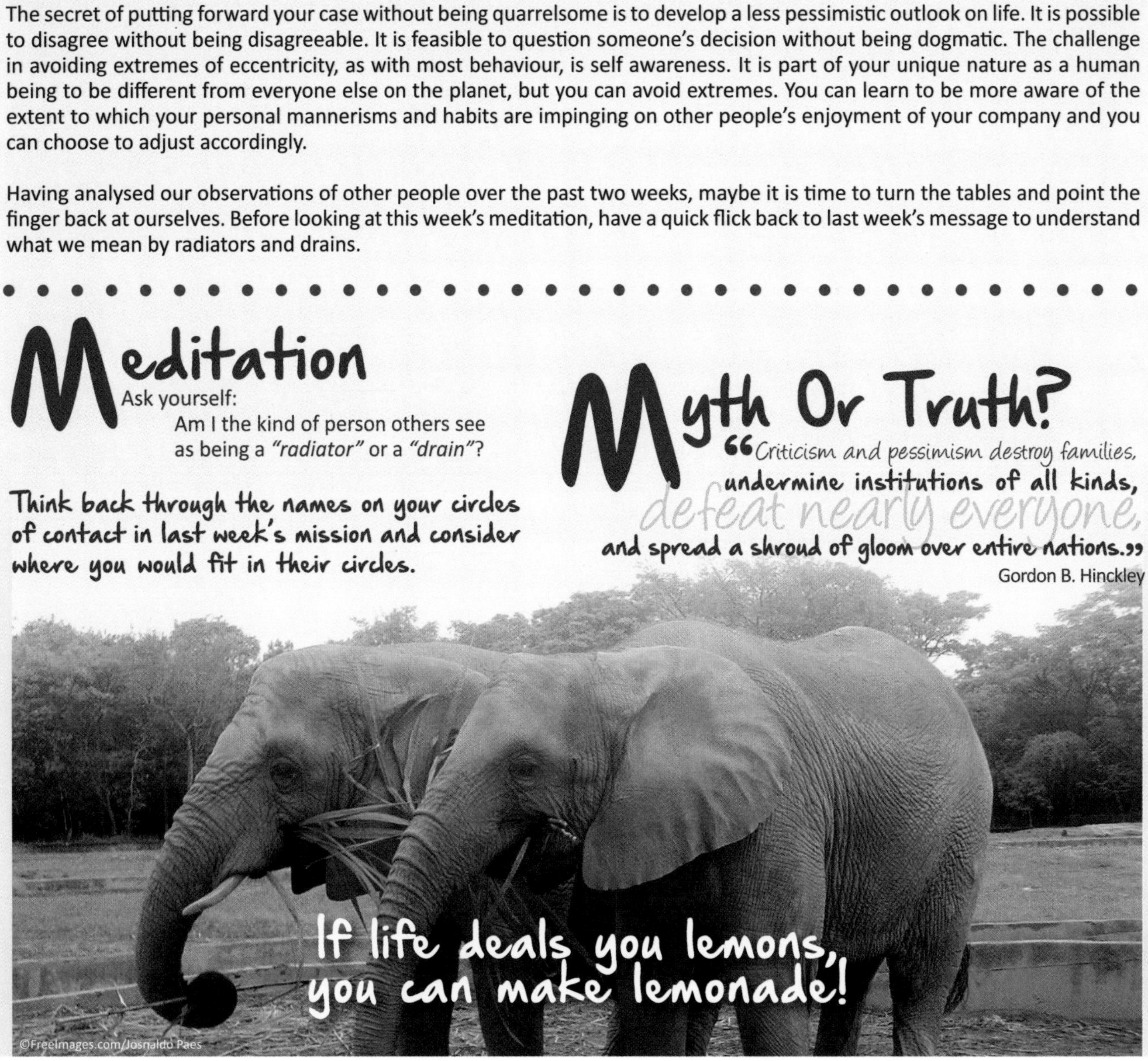

Mission "Quality AND Quantity" Q

WEEK 1: Your mission is to overcome any tendency to be quarrelsome.
Learning how to deal with disagreements will mean that it is no longer necessary to be quarrelsome. Remember, when we are quarrelsome we can become negative and pessimistic which are both destructive tendencies that can be avoided through good communication.

Three things we disagree on, which must have agreement in the near future:
1.

2.

3.

Three things we can continue to disagree on without harming the relationship:
1.

2.

3.

Now show each other what you have written and see if you agree that you disagree on those matters!!!

Next choose one from the list that must reach agreement soon and use the good communication skills guide to begin discussing the way forward. Don't be afraid to leave the conversation unfinished at any point, either with a set or an open ended time schedule for resuming the discussion later on. Often time limits on talking and making a plan to take a break before you even begin can be really helpful, as it gives time for reflection and seeing each other's point of view, and it stops the atmosphere getting too heated.

We have named this kind of taking a break in a disagreement "**parking**" it. The issue is safely off the road where it is not going to cause us to collide or crash. We both understand that we are processing the issues and giving each other space and will respond positively when it is time to re-open the discussion. In the meantime there is no need for either of us to jibe at the other or bring up the issue as a means of belittling or punishing the other person.

Use the coming week to develop your understanding of each other regarding the issue you have selected to address.

WEEK 2: Your mission is to recognise any quirkiness in yourself that it would be better to be free from.
Here are twelve characteristics of eccentricity. Some are not necessarily bad traits to possess. The health of your interaction with others depends on the extremity of your tendency towards certain combinations. So, as you read them through, rate your tendency towards each one on a scale of 1-5 and then give yourself a total out of 60. The higher your score, the more eccentric you tend to be! (1=less quirky/5=more quirky)

1 2 3 4 5 • Nonconforming
1 2 3 4 5 • Creative
1 2 3 4 5 • Strongly motivated by curiosity
1 2 3 4 5 • Idealistic: you want to make the world a better place and the people in it happier
1 2 3 4 5 • Happily obsessed with one or more hobbyhorses (preoccupations or favourite topics)
1 2 3 4 5 • Aware from early childhood that you are different
1 2 3 4 5 • Intelligent
1 2 3 4 5 • Opinionated and outspoken, convinced that you are right and that the rest of the world is out of step
1 2 3 4 5 • Non-competitive, not in need of reassurance or reinforcement from society
1 2 3 4 5 • Unusual in your eating habits and living arrangements
1 2 3 4 5 • Possessed of a mischievous sense of humour
1 2 3 4 5 • Not particularly interested in the opinions or company of other people, except in order to persuade them to your own (the correct) point of view

TOTAL:

Now ask your husband or wife to pick one trait which they think has an unhelpful effect on the marriage and discuss how some extra self awareness and some small changes could make a big difference.

Photography: Sue Roseblade

Macro Story

Ian and Elaine had been married for 32 years. The children had all grown up and moved away from home and life was beginning to feel a little easier, certainly less hectic. They felt they had done a good job as parents, in spite of their different temperaments and the way they would often argue about styles of discipline. There were lots of things they still disagreed about and Elaine had grown to expect that as soon as she put forward a suggestion of any sort, Ian would be more than likely to quash it with his pessimistic objections. She had learned to be fairly thick skinned, not taking his rejection of her enthusiasm quite so personally, because often, given time to mull things over, he would come round to her way of thinking in the end. But in the last year or so, it had come to annoy her more and more.

She puzzled over it, wondering how this must have always stood between them and how they had managed to live with it when trying to overcome far bigger issues than they had to deal with these days. Yet, in spite of all they had survived, she now didn't seem able to forgive him this negative behaviour any longer. She wondered whether it was because, having learned to deal with the bigger problems, it seemed incredibly petty that they still found themselves in opposition over smaller ones.

It had been on her mind for a while to ask him if they could discuss this difficulty..... and she had been trying to find a good moment to bring up the subject, hoping that if he wasn't busy thinking about the football fixtures or his next presentation for work, he would be able to give her his full attention. At last, one evening after dinner, the atmosphere seemed good and she attempted to approach the subject softly.

©iStockphoto.com/Daisy-Daisy

"I know you have a more cautious temperament than mine, and my liking for change and taking risks scares you sometimes, but do you think there's anything else between us that makes you almost instinctively say no to anything I suggest?" She paused, determined to stop at that, although the temptation to add justifying examples and emotional back up was very strong. The quiet turned into a long silence and as the second hand of the dining room clock ticked loudly on, her pulse thumped in time with it.

Eventually Ian did speak, not as defensively as Elaine had expected, and thoughts began to flow back and forth between them like a game of hide and seek. As they talked, the hour hand moved unnoticeably around the face of the clock, in contrast to the second hand's tour of duty during their initial silence. The couple became engrossed in unpacking Ian's past and one by one the pieces of the jigsaw were fitted into place.

Ian's father had died when he was only ten and he remembered his mother sitting the five of them down and telling them all how life was going to be from then on. He was the eldest and, for sure, he had taken the responsibility that had landed squarely on his shoulders, but nothing had come to him easily either then or since. There had been setbacks and disappointments aplenty, for all members of the family, hard times when the stiff upper lip had been a lesson well learned and emotions had been buried because no one taught anyone else how to communicate them safely. His recollection was that just as he hoped that life would give him a break, it didn't. His enemies had become the brown enveloped bills and car troubles and things that would break as soon as you looked at them.

Better not to go out for the day than to have to be towed home on the back of a truck..... Better not to lay a carpet in the lounge because the kids would bring mud in from the garden..... Better not to cut down the tree to get more light in the house because the stump would be ugly in the middle of the rockery..... Better not lend something because you might not get it back..... and so his mindset had become fixed. Change was an opportunity for things to go wrong. Having little meant there was less to lose. Not expecting good to come his way meant that he would experience fewer disappointments.

The realisation that dawned on Ian that evening, that his negative mindset had become a self fulfilling prophecy, was a revelation to him and such a relief to Elaine.

Change has since come about in small and gradual steps, but they have found the big difference is being able to talk and laugh about tensions and if when they still arise.

"I find it best to never interrupt my wife when she is making a mistake."

©FreeImages.com/Yamamoto Ortiz

Respect & Radiance

Message

When we give children credit for understanding just a little bit more than we really think they are capable of, they grow to meet our expectations. That is how they learn. If we speak to them as though they are still babies, then we teach them nothing. We have been astounded at the vocabulary our grandson has acquired through being chatted to and having his many questions answered in an adult manner. By the age of three he had grasped the concepts behind such words as 'similar' and 'complicated' and would use them in appropriate contexts himself. He has risen to the challenge of the language to which he has been exposed.

As adults we still have the same need to be gently stretched. When somebody believes in us, when they champion our cause, when they encourage us against all odds, we rise to meet the achievements and adopt the character qualities they perceive possible. This is the essence of respect: to see the good and to believe the best in a person. To be able to offer someone total respect, I must be secure in my own selfhood because I need to stop myself having defensive or self righteous responses to people's accidents, failures or momentary regressions into immature behaviour.

Again we see the truth of this most easily by looking at patterns of good parenting. The mother or father who is able to distract their toddler from a temper tantrum rather than launching headlong into battle, shows great wisdom. In a few years' time, with better reasoning skills, the approach may be different, but for now, while the child is still too young to process the emotional pain of a fierce conflict, the trauma of a crushed spirit has been avoided.

Many grown men and women who have suffered at the hands of very normal but less than perfect parenting will find themselves still reacting in immature ways to other people's imperfections, because they have never yet unburdened themselves of their own store of accumulated emotional pain from their childhood. This leaves them in a tricky position when it comes to offering or receiving respect. Considering that by nature we are all flawed to some degree, and in need of someone to be our own number one fan, when we get married the challenge is to fulfil that role for our husband or wife. Even when our spouse is not believing the best of us, the only successful approach for us is to believe the best about them. We have to see them as we would like them to be and to treat them as though they are wonderful already!

The Bible confronts husbands with the mission to present their wives 'radiant' and it challenges wives to so build their husbands' confidence that they become 'respected at the city gate' as they sit 'among the elders of the land'. Proverbs 31:23. Such radiance and good standing come through being respected and believed in. As we give our spouse this gift, which in the early years they perhaps don't deserve, we ourselves are rewarded: "He who loves his wife loves himself." (and vice versa?) Ephesians 5:28

R

Myth Or Truth?

No one can make you feel inferior without your consent.

Behind every good man, there is a great woman, (and vice versa)?

Meditation

Don't rub it in, rub it out!

Do you think there is any connection between respect and romance?
Write your own definition of each of the following making any appropriate links between them:

Respect is.....

Romance is.....

Radiance is.....

"Live so that when your children think of fairness, caring and integrity, they think of you."

H. Jackson Brown, Jr

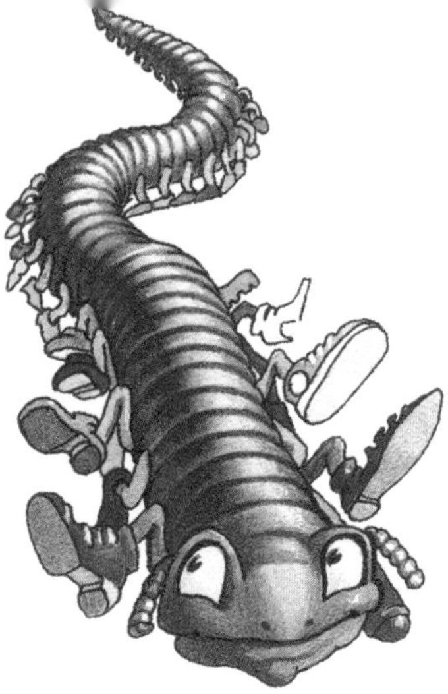

MUDDY FOOTPRINTS don't mean I don't love you, they just mean I FORGOT YOU WASHED THE FLOOR!

Micro Story

"I'm sure we aren't alone in that we often try speaking to each other from too far away in the house! Maybe one person thinks the other has finished talking and they head off to another room, missing a further piece of information. Sometimes one of us is close to the kettle or the washing machine and so although the distance isn't too great, there is too much interference to be able to hear. Really it's no big deal.

But, you know, for a long time it was part of the blame game we would play. As the 'listener' we would see it as an opportunity to 'play devil's advocate'. We would punish the 'speaker' with an annoyed attitude that pressed home our point that they should have known we were out of earshot. We'd make it obvious that they'd caused a real nuisance by making us have to return to the room, or come away from what we were doing, to listen.

Suddenly one day, we realised how stupid this was. We agreed that neither of us was speaking with the intention of winding up the other person. We came to understand that the listener would get annoyed because they believed that the speaker was already annoyed at not having been heard. Whether or not the speaker was the first to get cross, the listener's annoyance certainly aggravated the speaker, and so it was impossible to tell who was first to lose the plot!

We've now managed to stop believing the worst of each other when this happens and to start believing instead the truth that nobody meant it to happen out of spite. A soft answer really does turn away wrath!"

John

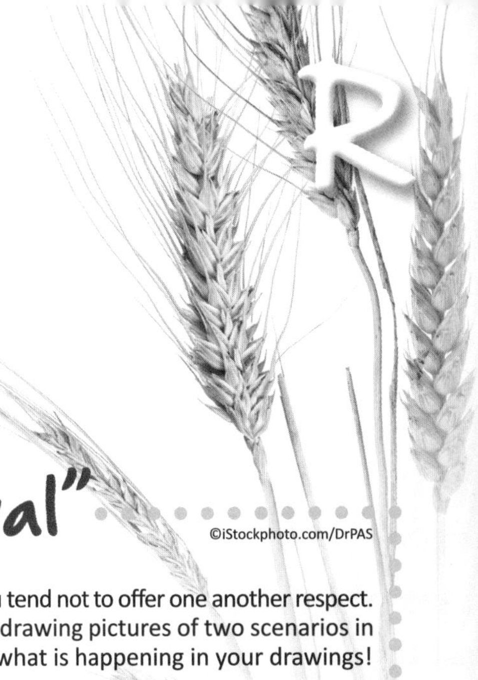

Mission "HarvestFestival"

WEEK 1: Your mission is to recognise situations in which you tend not to offer one another respect. Thinking back to the example in the micro story, have a quick game of Pictionary by drawing pictures of two scenarios in which respect tends to be lacking between you. Then see if your spouse can guess what is happening in your drawings!

1.	2.

Without accusing the other person of any lack of respect on their part, apologise for the ways in which you can see you fall short in these scenarios and then swap roles.

Be particularly on your toes in the coming week whenever a similar experience arises and aim to change your negative reactions for more loving and respectful ones.

WEEK 2: Your mission is to take on the task of making your spouse radiant this week! We've called this mission a 'harvest festival', because we hope you'll be gathering together all the resources you have for feeding your relationship! Your task is to use the technique of believing the best in every circumstance in order to inspire a moment of romance every day this week. It doesn't have to lead to sex; it is simply fostering closeness by meeting the need of the moment. That does take a bit of thinking through, because many of us have experienced going to great lengths to wine and dine our spouse, only to miss the mark completely.

If you can work out what is most needed on any particular day you could become the world's greatest romantic with the world's most radiant spouse! Here's a list to get your mind in gear, but there may be other more specific matters to which you need to attend:

Pay respectful compliments on their appearance or achievements • Help them to 'pick up' after a hard day •Kiss them passionately with no underlying agenda • Pay full attention to their conversation and listen with good body language • Don't filter out their chat • Help them with chores or paperwork • Text or phone them in your break • Hold their hand when you are out together • Plan to do something that will make them really laugh • Hold their gaze and tell them you love them • Empathise with any problems they encounter •Take them out for a walk / a meal / a movie • Send them a card through the post • Make some progress with a task or project that has been on hold for ages • Cuddle up close when you watch TV • Only choose programmes you know they will enjoy • Apologise for any insensitivities that have upset them • Resolve or 'park' any disagreements • Touch them affectionately as you pass each other round the house • Eat dinner at the table together whenever you can • Forgive them for the thing you seem unable to put behind you • Hold them close for a long time • Hurry home and let them know when you're on your way • Buy flowers / chocolate / beer/ take away • Organise a date night

Add your own ideas...

Study your spouse carefully if you are not sure what they most need, and try out different options from the list. You will soon know if you are doing what's needed by the responses you receive..... and by their gradually increasing radiance. If you make progress this week, turn it into a lifetime project!

Secrets & Surprises

©FreeImages.com/Korry.B

Message

Some of us love surprises, whilst others of us may not be so keen. How we react will depend on a number of different factors, but one of the most important is likely to be the level of trust we are able to accrue. Trust builds slowly as the product of our experiences. If you like surprises, you probably have happy memories of ways in which people have given you unexpected gifts or planned enjoyable events for you in the past. They will have taken the trouble to make sure that they knew your likes and dislikes and will have understood what would make you happy. If we are going to create a surprise, we do have to first keep our plan a secret. So, in that scenario, secrets can have a positive place in a relationship.

However, deliberately keeping secrets that are not destined to turn into surprises will be damaging in almost every case. Information that is not shared will put up barriers between us and will lead us away from oneness and towards superficiality. We will find ourselves hiding the truth not only from other people, but also from ourselves. We can become experts in creating an image of ourselves that does not represent who we really are.

Instead of secret-keeping, we do well to make ourselves accountable to one another, allowing our spouse to help us to live up to our best intentions and highest values. John Wesley called it **"watching over one another in love"**.

Myth Or Truth?

Are the following observations of human behaviour true for you in any way?

"We keep temptation a secret because we want the option of giving in to it undiscovered." John Ortberg, Everybody's Normal Till You Get to Know Them

"We usually tell the truth until it is costly and then we trade truth for peace." John Ortberg, Everybody's Normal Till You Get to Know Them

The way that my wife is acting toward me says more about me than it does about her.

Honesty is the best policy.

©FreeImages.com/rebirth

S

Mission "Stumbling Blocks to Stepping Stones"

WEEK 1: Your mission is to confess anything that should no longer be kept secret. Whatever it is that you need to tell your husband or wife, it will most likely have already come into your mind as you are reading this. But take a few minutes in quietness to think whether there is also anything less obvious.

Now take your courage in both hands and write your confession as a letter to your spouse. You may not want a record of it here in THE MAGAZINE, so use a separate piece of paper that can be burned or shredded later. Either read your confession aloud or give it to your spouse to read to themselves, whichever is more comfortable for you. Remember as you do this, that you are giving the gift of freedom not only to them, but also to yourself. You are also making it a whole lot easier for them, if they need to confess something to you.

If, after searching your heart, you have in all honesty no secrets to declare, write a letter anyway appreciating the honesty and integrity you share, and perhaps remembering back to past confessions which bought you your freedom, listing the many blessings you have enjoyed as a result.

WEEK 2: Your mission is to plan a surprise that your spouse will love! Not everybody likes the same form of surprise, so think about your husband or wife's personality, the kind of things they would really enjoy without getting stressed in any way, and the advance warning they will need to maximise their enjoyment. A surprise doesn't have to be kept secret right up until it happens. In many cases it can work better to make our plan and then choose a good time to tell our spouse in advance of the event. That way they can enjoy looking forward to it and preparing for it, which many people prefer.

©FreeImages.com/Lesley Mackin

Write your plan in answer to the following questions on a separate piece of paper, and tuck it in your wallet or purse, until it comes to fruition.

- What will you plan?
- What steps will you need to take to make it happen?
- Who will be involved?
- When would be the best time to tell your husband or wife?

©FreeImages.com/Svilen Milev

©FreeImages.com/Mario Alberto Magallanes Trejo

"I only kept my golf club membership a secret, because I thought you liked surprises!"

©FreeImages.com/Viktors Kozers

Micro Story

"My story is that I almost got myself into an affair. I never meant the thing to happen, but I was doing some work for a young widow and spending quite a bit of time at her house with her around to make me drinks and give me lunch. At home things had grown quite dull. There was a lot of work to be done there as well and the kids took any spare time we had. So to be away from it all and having a laugh and a chat with this friend of ours felt enjoyable, if not downright sexy.

More and more I would look forward to each day that I was there. You know how things develop, so I don't need to give you all the detail. Anyway, I was feeling really bad towards my wife, and I knew I didn't really want things to go wrong for us and the kids. What to do?

In the end I plucked up courage to grab a few minutes on our own – and I told my wife what was going on. Well – it didn't go as badly as you'd expect. Do you know..... as I told her my secret it was as if the bubble burst and suddenly I could see the bigger picture more clearly. The feelings I'd been having largely disappeared. It certainly didn't seem as exciting any more and I knew for sure I wouldn't have wanted it to go any further. It was as if keeping the secret from my wife was in itself the exciting thing, rather than the prospect of an affair. Guilty speculations about how I would handle a sexual encounter, if it had got that far, had been eating away at me giving me moments of panic and a great deal of stress.

My wife was of course shocked by what I told her, but she later told me that it said a lot about the quality of our relationship for me to have made the choice to tell her and she seemed honoured and encouraged. It took a while for us to work through it and come out the other side, but deciding to tell her that secret was one of the best choices I have made in our marriage."

Scott (aged 42)

S

"Marriage is the hardest thing you will ever do. The secret is removing divorce as an option. Anybody who gives themselves that option will get a divorce."

Will Smith
(11 years into his second marriage)

Model

"A warning from my experience: be careful with your choice of surprise gifts. I was given a helicopter paperweight from work in recognition of some target or other that had been achieved within the department. Arriving home, I carelessly got it out of my bag and handed it to Sue, with the words, "Here, I thought you might like this!" Unfortunately for me, it had completely bypassed my radar that the box looked incredibly like something from an expensive jewellery shop. It was sleek and black with a springy hinge and no writing on the outside. Sue opened it excitedly, only to have the sparkle in her eyes turn first to disappointment and then to rage when she discovered its surprise contents. My attempts to diffuse the ensuing tension with humour were only met with increased annoyance!"

John

Meditation

In the book of James, the Bible says that we have a strong tendency to look at ourselves in the mirror and then go away and immediately forget what we look like. Our husband or wife can act like a mirror for us, as they reflect back to us the vibes we give off, either by their positive affirmation of the good or their disapproval of the bad. Consider for a few minutes how able you are to read your husband or wife's behaviour towards you as a reflection of your own level of maturity.

Thoughts & Transformation

Message

Our thought life plays a huge part in the development of both our personality and our character. Whilst it is true that we are born with certain predispositions, much of who we are is formed by the way we process everything that happens to us and around us. Over the years our thought patterns develop into mindsets which can become very difficult to change, as our personality and our behaviour link into them, making us who we are at a very deep level of our psyche. In particular we are affected by the methods we adopt for processing our emotions because, if we are not careful, dependence on our feelings can end up driving much of our thinking down some very unhelpful pathways.

If we are going to be able to thwart this downward spiral into negativity, especially as we meet the challenges of later life, we need to learn self control and to recognise how to master our emotions by learning to think in positive ways. This is basic and popular psychology, but it isn't always easy to put into practice. In our experience transformation is a lifelong process that needs our full co-operation and the gentle encouragement of a husband or wife who will bear with us every step of the way.

Meditation

Spend a few minutes thinking through the following train of thought:

"Life is difficult because....."

After 5 minutes, how are you now feeling?

Now spend 5 minutes thinking this thought:

"Life is wonderful because....."

How do you feel now?

Photography: Sue Roseblade

Myth Or Truth?

A leopard cannot change its spots.

T

"....as he thinks in his heart, so is he." Proverbs 23:7 NKJV

Mission "Think Tank"

Photography: Sue Roseblade

WEEK 1: Your mission is to understand the extent to which your thoughts control your feelings. Here are 20 thoughts and some possible corresponding emotions. Your task is to draw lines to match each thought to the most likely feeling it would create in you:

1. "Things will no doubt turn out for the best."
2. "If this continues, I won't know what to do."
3. "Why does this sort of thing always happen to me?"
4. "I can't believe that he could've done such a thing!"
5. "My ideas never seem to count for anything."
6. "It's not my fault, but I wish it hadn't happened like that."
7. "I don't believe she'll always be like this."
8. "His ideas are never thought through well enough."
9. "I can't believe that I could have done such a thing!"
10. "I'm so looking forward to seeing what will happen."
11. "I really wish I hadn't been so foolish."
12. "It is wonderful just to be together."
13. "How can people be so unaware of what's going on?"
14. "I can't believe that you could have done such a thing!"
15. "I have worked really hard at that today."
16. "Even if I'm in a mess, the sun is shining today."
17. "If it wasn't for her, I'd not be in this mess."
18. "Phew, the pressure's off at last!"
19. "Friends come easily to her, she's so outgoing and sociable."
20. "Even though I was foolish, people were kind towards me."

Fear
Hope
Contentment
Self pity
Rejection
Anticipation
Sadness
Optimism
Resentment
Anger
Happiness
Shock
Triumph
Contempt
Remorse
Satisfaction
Disapproval
Pleasure
Envy
Relief

Interestingly, Note how the same thought can provoke different emotions when applied to others or to ourselves!!!

Share your answers with each other and discuss any differences.

For which of the numbered pairs above do you feel you exercise most self control:_______ least self control:________?

Affirm each other's self control wherever you see it working well and commit to helping each other to improve in your less good areas, without patronising or being critical. Tell each other how you would find that kind of help easiest to receive when future instances arise.

WEEK 2: Your mission is to plan a transformation strategy for your thought life.
In the coming week, be ready to recognise any incident that triggers a negative emotion. When alerted by a feeling, immediately write down the thoughts that accompany it. Keep THE MAGAZINE handy and enter your responses here when you have time to reflect on what happened. Then carefully plan a more positive thought pattern that would change your focus and enable you to take better control. It may be either a reasoned argument against your previous thoughts, or simply a short phrase that you can repeat to yourself over and over until your mindset is changed. Bible verses can be of great value in this context. Why not try a word search on www.biblegateway.com to find something applicable?

Feeling:	→ Thoughts:	→ Alternative thinking:

Macro Story

"For much of my early adult life I was aware that my thoughts were under my own control. I knew I had a choice about where I focussed my attention. It was possible, although never easy, to curtail a train of thought that was leading me into negative thinking or a bad attitude. What I did not recognise was the intricate connection between thoughts and feelings. It seemed to me that thoughts occurred in the brain and feelings in the gut and that there was therefore a huge gap between the two. Because I could succeed in not dwelling on certain thoughts if I chose, they seemed somehow more external, less the real me, than my feelings which I felt powerless to control.

If someone wounded me, I felt hurt. If someone wronged me, I felt indignant and revengeful. If I was betrayed or abandoned, there was rejection, loneliness, fear and self pity. I didn't ask for these feelings, they just came. I didn't believe anyone could choose how to feel. Emotions were, I thought, just the natural reaction to things that happen to us daily. As negative feelings beset me time and time again they seemed to determine the kind of person I was. They seemed to tell me that I was this self pitying, lonely, revengeful person, rather than the generous, outgoing and considerate character that existed in my mind's eye. When other people witnessed, and reacted against, the attitudes my feelings created, it only led to more disappointment with who I was. As a result, I quite disliked myself and felt as though I had a measure of split personality. I would constantly be beating myself up as I lived with a false burden of guilt that I didn't know was unnecessary.

One day, when standing at the sink, and fuming about something a friend had done which had really annoyed me, I heard a thought quite clearly come into my mind above the internal clamour of the unending arguments with self. It was just five short words: "your thoughts control your feelings". It was simple and clear and I understood its implications immediately. I don't often hear God speaking to me directly, but the way that thought came, and brought with it the power that was needed to change me, I am convinced that it was Him intervening in my muddled arguments. It was the jolt I needed to realise that I was

not after all at the mercy of my feelings, and that if I actually did control my thoughts, then I could also master the emotions.

I recognised that, although I knew I could stop thinking unhelpful thoughts, frequently I didn't choose to do that. So, once I had given a thought house room and it had then instigated a negative emotion, I would allow the emotion to drive more negative thinking and it would become a vicious circle. Gradually I learned it was not enough just to try to stop the negative thoughts because the effort involved meant I was still focussing on them..... and therefore thinking them!

A much more helpful solution was to think about something positive. I found that by filling my mind completely with alternative, positive thoughts there was no space for the negatives to return. I'm sure you can guess the outcome; the unhealthy emotions disappeared and I was happier.

I am still daily in the process of applying the principle to my life, but whenever I do, it works! Sometimes it is still a wrench to give up the comfort of wallowing in the hurts and railing against the injustices, but the more battles I win, the more encouraged I am that the real me is actually the person I want to be, not the person I don't like.”

Sue

Photography: Sue Roseblade

©FreeImages.com/sitesyrup ©FreeImages.com/CJLUC

Umbrellas & Umbilical Cords

©iStockphoto.com/Dean Mitchell

Message

An essential characteristic of the human condition is that we need to belong. Relationships are crucial to our sense of well being. However, we also need freedom to act independently. These two contrasting needs have to be carefully balanced as we form attachments. Part of the responsibility of relationship is that we take on the role of acting as witnesses of each other's lives. Part of the privilege of relationship is that when all the minute details of our lives are witnessed, they become meaningful.

In the 2004 film "Shall We Dance?" the wife, played by Susan Sarandon, describes this privilege: "We need a witness to our lives. There's a billion people on the planet..... I mean, what does any one life really mean? But in a marriage, you're promising to care about everything: the good things, the bad things, the terrible things, the mundane things..... all of it, all of the time, every day. You're saying 'Your life will not go unnoticed because I will notice it. Your life will not go unwitnessed because I will be your witness.'"

Psychiatrist, Frank Pittman, endorses the same concept: "For most people, a life lived alone, with passing strangers or passing lovers, is incoherent and ultimately unbearable. Someone must be there to know what we have done for those we love."

In order to respect that our husband or wife has been charged with this duty, we need to place ourselves under the umbrella of protection that their promise of commitment offers us. There is a very natural, and yet at the same time a very spiritual, process of accountability that comes about when we submit ourselves voluntarily under the covering of their vow to stick with us for better or for worse. We permit our spouse a certain measure of authority to speak into our lives because they are our witness and we accept the fact that they will guide and channel and redirect us from time to time. It is through this process that we develop maturity of character.

In order for us to function well in response to this challenge, it is extremely important that we sever the remains of our umbilical cord. Obviously we are speaking metaphorically here, but the meaning is clear. Growing up under the umbrella of our parents or carers, they were for many years our chief witnesses. Because of our accountability to them, and their authority over us, we naturally would have sought their approval as our top priority. When we establish a married relationship we move out from under their umbrella and the umbilical ties are cut for good. We can (and should) still maintain a close relationship with them, but its future will be on the basis of friendship rather than parenting. Our new covering should be from our husband or wife, with the husband shouldering the chief accountability for the health of the relationship.

As we look around in today's culture, we can't help but see the difficulty and confusion in extended family relationships, often caused by casual short term relationships and couples who choose to live together without committing to marriage. Many parents don't mean to overstep the mark, but without the defined "leaving and cleaving" of the marriage ceremony and the opportunity that it creates for the whole community to stand together to 'witness' the newly formed order of relationship, boundaries remain unclear and it is easy to offend and be offended. The couple themselves often upset each other too as they continue to draw more heavily on the witness of members of the family than on their partner. Relatives and friends are left to read between the lines and couples can find themselves pulling in different directions for the covering they need, because they have not consented to the commitment necessary for receiving it from each other.

This week's micro story reveals one gentleman's interesting take on the meaning of commitment, as he talks to his hairdresser.....

Micro Story

“I was at the barber's last month and overheard the following conversation:

Hairdresser (making small talk):
Going anywhere nice for your holidays this year?

Gent:
Don't know yet. The girlfriend wants to save up to get married. So I don't think we'll have much cash floating around.

Hairdresser (instantly in pink and fluffy chick flick dream world):
Aw, that's so nice. How long have you been together?

Gent:
I guess around 7 years or so. Don't know why we can't just stay as we are. It seems to work fine for me. But she says I'm afraid of commitment.

Hairdresser (daring to boldly go where no man has gone before):
Are you?

Gent:
Nah..... I've already got a 30 year mortgage, a 5 year car loan, lifetime membership at the gym and 3 kids, so I'm a pretty committed kind of guy.

Hairdresser (genuinely bemused):
What are you afraid of then?

Gent:
I already feel under the thumb..... think how much worse that could get if I become part of her family! Sometimes even now it feels like I'm part of her whole network of other relationships. I'm better off being my own man. I like the idea of just looking after number one.

Hairdresser (getting annoyed, but trying to sound sympathetic):
But you've been together a long time, you must care about each other a lot.

Gent:
Sure we do, but I don't want to have to share everything with her. A guy's got to have some secrets and hang on to his freedom as best he can.

Hairdresser (looking at the back of his hair and daring herself to take the guard off the clippers):
What about the kids? Don't you think that committing to marriage is security for them?

Gent:
Can't see how that would help, they're not her kids!

Hairdresser (handing him the mirror and removing the plastic cape):
Well enjoy your holiday, sir. I hope you don't end up going by yourself!”

Harry

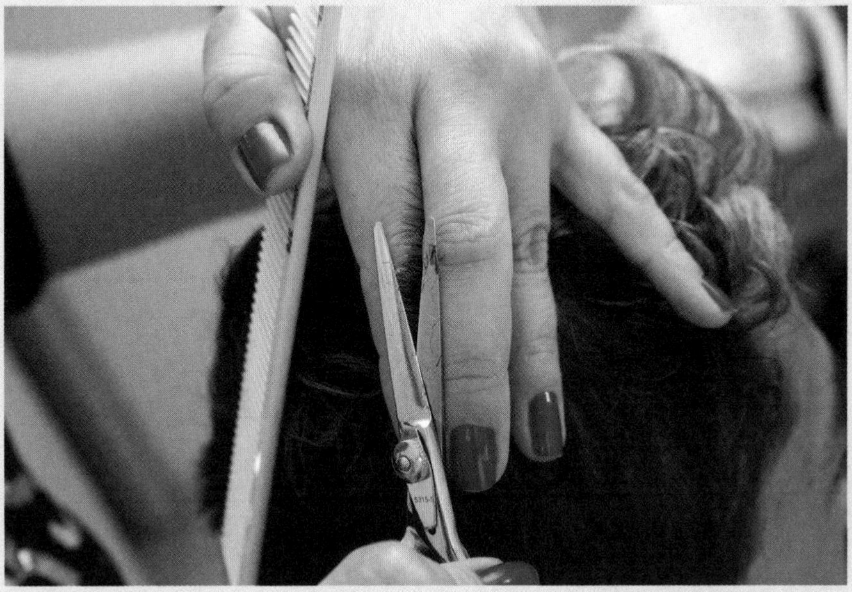

©FreeImages.com/Flavio Takemoto

Meditation

“I didn't marry you because you were perfect. I didn't even marry you because I loved you. I married you because you gave me a promise. That promise made up for your faults. And the promise I gave you made up for mine. Two imperfect people got married and it was the promise that made the marriage. And when our children were growing up, it wasn't a house that protected them; and it wasn't our love that protected them - it was that promise.”

Thornton Wilder, The Skin of Our Teeth

“Marriage is a promise. Not just between the couple but to the community at large, to generations past and to those yet to be born.”

Heritage.org

Mission "Witness Protection"

WEEK 1: Your mission is to evaluate the importance of the traditional marriage vows and to reassess your commitment to one another.

Traditionally marriage vows ran almost exactly like this:

I take you…
to have and to hold
from this day forward,
for better, for worse,
for richer, for poorer,
in sickness and in health,
to love and to cherish,
till death us do part.

Today, under the influence of technology, films and social media, for some couples they may look more like this:

If you make me feel loved, then I'll marry you.
If you satisfy me sexually, then I'll marry you.
If you treat me with respect, then I'll marry you.
If you make me happy, then I'll marry you.
If you fulfil my needs, then I'll marry you.
If you like what I like, then I'll marry you.
If you make something of yourself, then I'll marry you.
If you don't do things that get on my nerves, then I'll marry you.

Many couples like to expand or change the traditional phrasing to make them more personal. It is good to express our continuing commitment to one another in language that is clear and meaningful to us personally, provided that we are not lowering our level of commitment in the process.

A helpful way of thinking about vows is that whereas a promise can only be either kept or broken, a vow is a goal that we work towards, thus setting us up to succeed, rather than dooming us to failure.

Read through the following expansive statements and tick all those with which you would like to agree:

1. We are together for life. ☐
2. Our relationship is more important than my own happiness. ☐
3. My responsibilities come before my rights. ☐
4. My job is to protect you. ☐
5. I will care for you through any sickness to the best of my ability. ☐
6. I forgive you all your imperfections. ☐
7. Our incompatibilities are a challenge but not a problem. ☐
8. Selflessness is my goal. ☐
9. I trust you to tell me everything. ☐
10. Our relationship will always be my number one priority. ☐
11. I will not keep secrets from you. ☐
12. I am happy to share all my wealth and possessions with you. ☐
13. I will not share my emotional needs inappropriately with others. ☐
14. I choose not to engage with any pornographic material or fantasies. ☐
15. When we disagree I will respect and work towards understanding your views. ☐
16. I intend to speak well of you to everyone, always. ☐
17. I will see the good in you and believe the best of you. ☐
18. I will not flirt with others or put myself in compromising situations. ☐
19. I will help you to reach your goals and achieve your dreams. ☐
20. I will be faithful to you emotionally and sexually every day of my life. ☐
21. Divorce is not an option. ☐

Add any more of your own here:

When you have both had time to reflect on your ticked list, sit or stand together and declare each of your ticked statements to one another as affirmation of the covering you continue to offer each other. Decide whether one of you will declare all their statements first or whether you will take it in turns.

Circle one vow that needs you to "pull your socks up" and make its challenge your focus for this week. Write its number here as a reminder: ____

U

WEEK 2: Your mission is to assess the impact of your relationship on your family, friends, colleagues and community and their impact on you.

As they come to your mind, enter names of those you know in appropriate boxes according to how you see the relationship functioning.

Too dependent on:	Too independent of:	Interfering:	Connected to:
Supported by:	Supportive of:	Accountable to:	Under the authority of:

Discuss the following questions with each other:

1. How does your level of commitment to each other have a bearing on these other relationships?

2. Are there any unclear boundaries between you and your family, friends, colleagues or neighbours and can you work out why that might be?

3. Do you believe that your relationship has an impact on or makes a contribution to your community? If so what does that look like in practice?

4. Which of the relationships you have put in the boxes above requires most improvement? How you could help protect each other and how you could make some positive changes?

Myth Or Truth?

Do you agree or disagree that.....

“The truth is, you can't 'practise' marriage. Marriage is a permanent commitment. And you'll never know what the other person will do if you get cancer or lose your job until it happens years (perhaps even decades) down the road. That's part of the risk—part of the adventure. That's why part of the marriage vow says, “for better or for worse, in sickness and in health.”"

Felicia Alvarez www.crosswalk.com 6/5/2014

Sean Lowe of The Bachelor said his counsellor showed him that “a woman's heart is delicate, that it's her husband's job to guard, protect, and cherish her heart.”

I've installed the new firewall. It will protect you from **viruses**, infections, **worms**, crashes, upgrades, downloads, clean ups, clear outs, **scams**, spam, *jam*, ham and all *unsolicited advertising* or criminal activity. It should also protect me from aggravating emails from your parents.

©FreeImages.com/Ben Smith

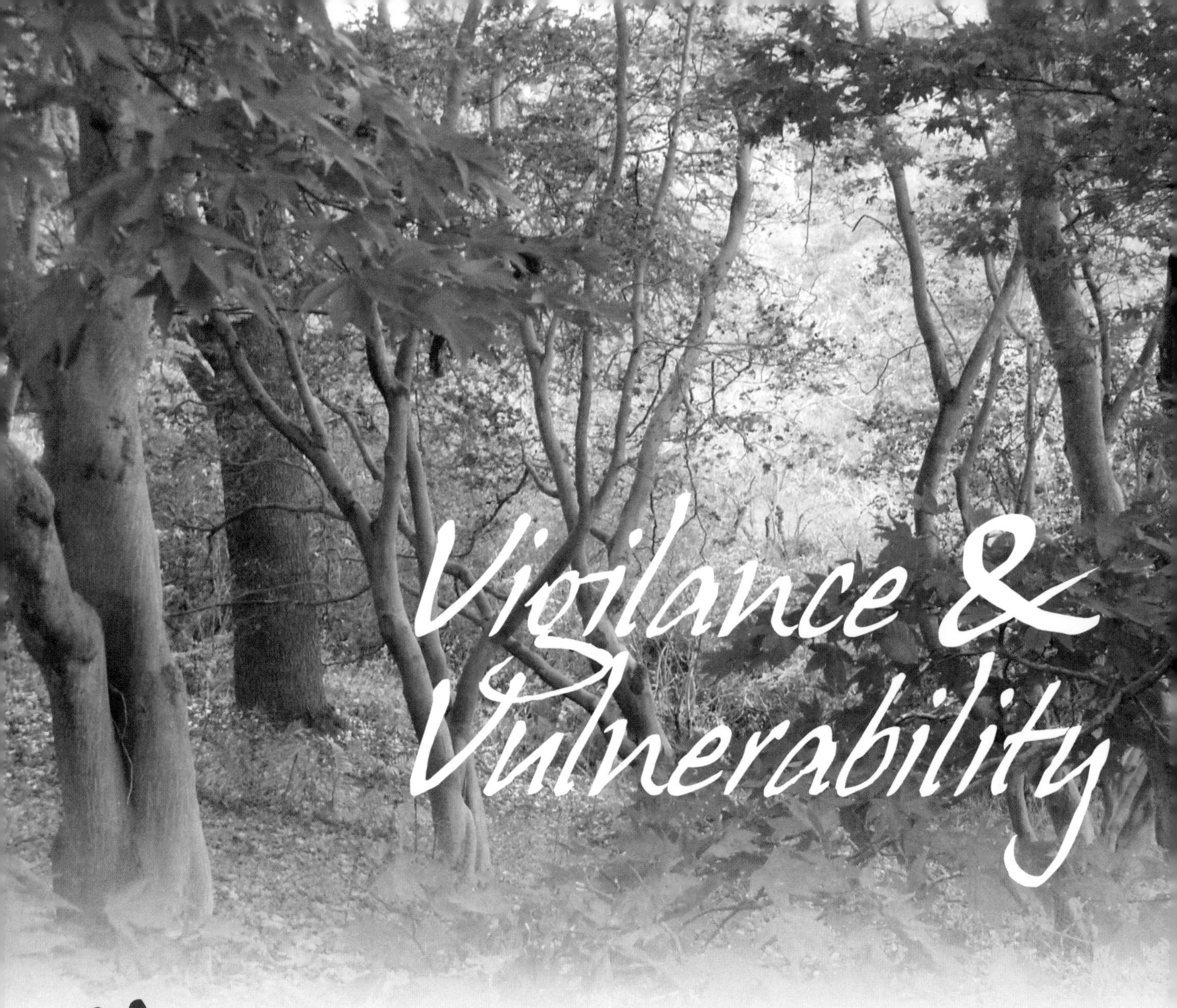

Vigilance & Vulnerability

Message

Vigilance is a key element of a healthy relationship. Its Oxford Dictionary definition is: 'The action or state of keeping careful watch for possible danger or difficulties.' More simply it means to keep an eye on things. The mistake is to presume that because everything was OK yesterday, that it will be OK today as well.

There's a popular joke in which a man says during his first upset with his new wife after making their recent wedding vows, "I've told you I love you. If anything changes, I'll let you know!" He will not make a vigilant husband with that philosophy! In fact if he holds to that mentality for any length of time, then very quickly there will be changes between them, and not likely for the better! Love is not a feeling that comes and goes through no fault of our own, it is an activity that has to be practised daily and its effects monitored and built upon.

Even when we are vigilant in monitoring the mood between us, why is it that the person we love the most, is often the one we seem to hurt the most? This question brings us to the connection between our two words this week. The definition of our second word, vulnerability, describes this state as being 'exposed to the possibility of being attacked or harmed, either physically or emotionally'.

The only means of developing a close connection with other human beings is to open up to them: to expose ourselves. That makes us vulnerable. Allowing someone to love us is therefore a brave and scary step to take and needs to be backed by a trust that our spouse won't trample on or crush our spirit. If we are vigilant in building that trust, then our closeness will flourish, but if we are lazy then our husband or wife will be forced into an uncomfortable position which they haven't chosen for themselves and will probably resort to either protecting themselves or punishing us.

"We have to be vulnerable if we want more courage..... how can we let ourselves be seen if shame has terrified us of what other people might think?"

Daring Greatly by Brené Brown

Why does vulnerability matter in your marriage? It matters because it is in itself an act of love. It says to your husband or wife that you have nothing to hide. It says you are willing to be accepted for who you really are, not who you would like to be. It unknowingly gives your spouse the permission they need to show their true self in return and to overcome their own fears of not being accepted for who they are. Without vulnerability there can be no emotional intimacy. Without emotional intimacy most women find physical intimacy difficult.

Photography: Sue Roseblade

Myth Or Truth?

Women crave a oneness which is only achieved through openness.
Men are happy to settle for peace.
This makes women more vulnerable than men and therefore more easily hurt.

Micro Story

Lauren, aged 42, tells her story:

“We don’t really argue these days, but don’t take that as a sign that we’re doing well. I don’t say what I really feel because I’m afraid of losing Mike’s approval or being ridiculed by him. I depend so much on his acceptance of me, in order to be able to give myself to him unconditionally, so it becomes a vicious circle between us. I sometimes won’t open up to him these days because so often he has hurt me or let me down in the past. He senses when I am shutting down and jibes at me all the more. It always seems to turn out that it’s my fault in the end. Then he tells me he doesn’t understand why I have such low self esteem, why I beat myself up so much. He asks why I can’t just let things go more easily. He can move on, so why can’t I?

Anyway, I was at the computer the other week and stuck on a task I hadn’t tried before. He’s cleverer than me when it comes to that sort of thing, but even he sometimes has to work it through bit by bit with the on line help. On this occasion the help menu was being no help at all, so I had no choice but to ask him. He breezed in confidently, delighted to have been asked, grabbed the mouse from me and started telling me what to do.

He hardly took a breath. I think that was so I didn’t have a moment to ask a question, just in case he couldn’t answer it! He rushed on so fast that I couldn’t keep up with what he was doing. A few times he changed tack mid sentence, when something on the screen didn’t do what he thought it would. That made it even harder to follow what he was doing. Finally when he got the result we wanted, he quit the application and gave me back the mouse saying, “Right now show me you can do it yourself”.

Of course I struggled and he thought I was acting dumb on purpose to make it look like he wasn’t a good teacher. He was annoyed that I hadn’t listened, and just thought I was being defensive when I tried to tell him I had needed to ask a question. I don’t know if I will invite him to help me again.”

Lauren

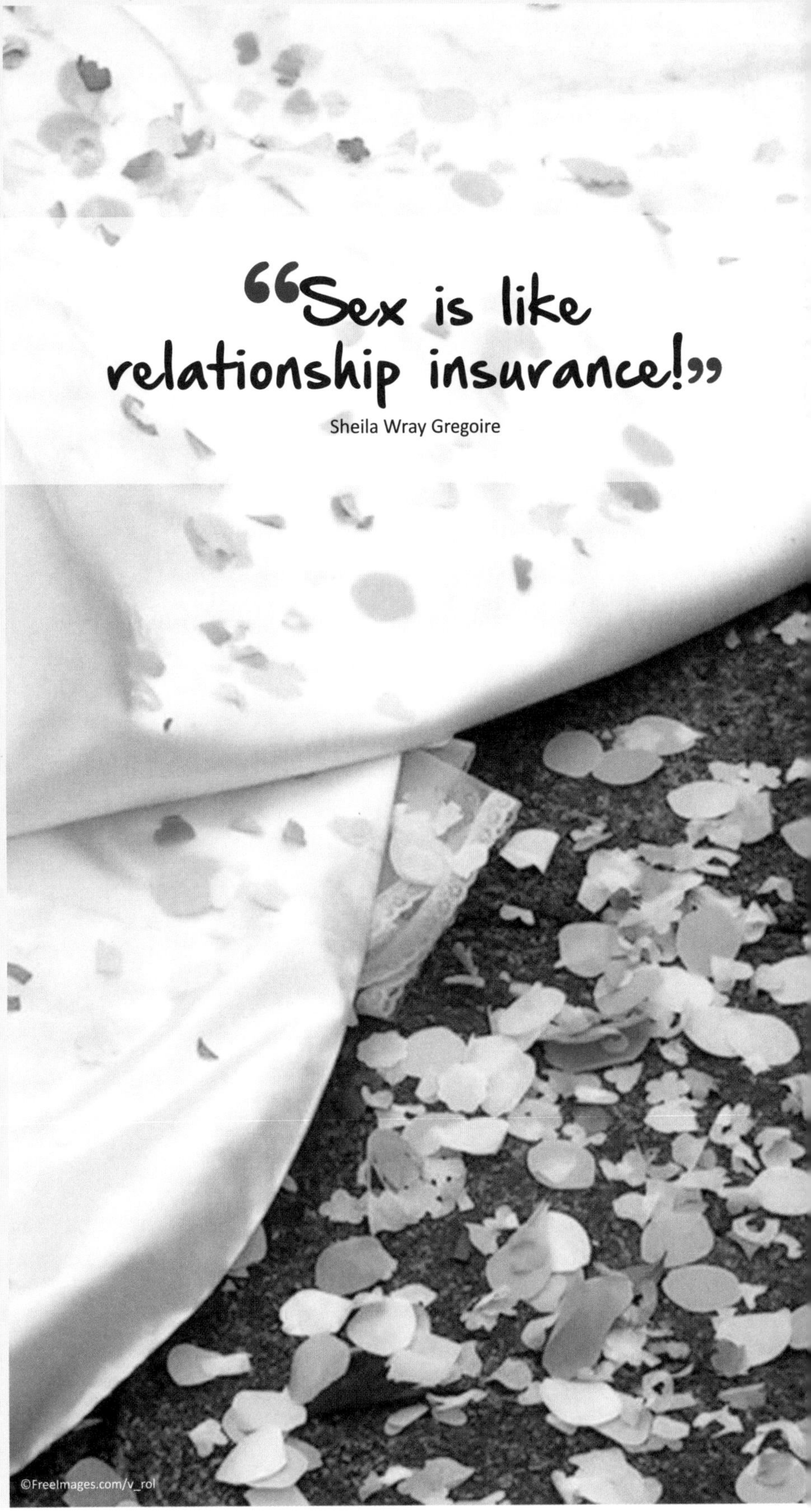

“Sex is like relationship insurance!”

Sheila Wray Gregoire

The price of liberty is eternal vigilance.

©FreeImages.com/Nancy Brown

©iStockphoto.com/Dennis Cox

"Our marriage turned out to be a damp squib. My wife blames it on me being too in love with my job!"

Mission "Watch and Learn"

WEEK 1: Your mission is to monitor your spouse's behaviour this week, being vigilant in detecting any changes. We have found it helpful to do this using the acronym: W A R M and to think, not only in terms of emotional behaviour, but to see how we would use this in context of our finances as well. Using finance as an analogy helps us to see why this kind of monitoring is necessary and how it also helps relationally.

	RELATIONAL APPLICATION	FINANCIAL ANALOGY
W IS FOR WATCH	Be aware of change in actions or demeanour.	Look on line at balance of the account.
A IS FOR ASSESS	Think back, looking for any reasons that could have caused the change.	Discover why the account is overdrawn.
R IS FOR REACT	Be proactive, feed their emotional needs. Take time out of routine to be together.	Stop spending and invest.
M IS FOR MONITOR	Stay focussed and in tune. Avoid being distracted by life crowding in.	Check the account daily.

Adopt the acronym WARM this week and use it as a tool to help you be vigilant in respect of your spouse's emotional health.

©FreeImages.com/IDFIX Design

V

Meditation

"Keep your heart with all vigilance; for from it flow the springs of life."

Proverbs 4:23 RSV

Is it possible to be vigilant in looking after our own heart at the same time as looking after our spouse's heart?
In what ways do you think you do this?

WEEK 2: Your mission is to confess any concerns you have about your vulnerability.

Vulnerability is where relationship begins:

"Vulnerability is the birthplace of everything we are hungry for." Dr. Brené Brown

It is also the crown that it achieves:

"Vulnerability is the cornerstone of confidence." Oprah Winfrey

Our willingness to be vulnerable will grow in proportion to our level of trust. Trust is a slow growing tree, whose sturdiness cannot be accelerated, so don't expect to whizz through to the third section of this list if your relationship is young or has been through troubled times recently.

These acts of love require increasing vulnerability as you move through the three sections, although depending on your personality you may judge some in section 1 harder or some in section 3 easier to accomplish. Tick those that you know you wouldn't have any difficulty with, and move on to those that are more challenging to you. Pick one which represents a small or medium measure of risk to you and act on it this week.

SECTION 1 – LOW RISK		SECTION 2 – MEDIUM RISK		SECTION 3 – HIGH RISK	
Share a highlight from your day.		Be honest about a regret that you have.		Admit to something you don't enjoy about sex.	
Share a disappointment.		Write a list of your biggest fears and share it with your spouse.		Tell the truth about something you have been covering up for a long time.	
Dare to ask for help with something that your spouse is better at than you.		Spend a weekend being completely you: No make up? No masks?		Confess an attraction to another person or a fantasy about someone you idolise.	
Write about one of your best qualities and how it makes you feel. Read it to your spouse.		Humble yourself next time you are contradicted and accept you could possibly be wrong!		Disclose something you are ashamed of from before you met your spouse.	
Empathise instead of competing if your spouse complains about tiredness/stress.		Next time your spouse puts you down/mocks you/criticises you, say nothing at all.		Write a letter to your spouse explaining the reasons behind your feelings of rejection.	
Show compassion to your spouse in a situation where you don't feel they deserve it.		Ask your spouse to tell you something that annoys them about you and try hard to change.		Instigate a drastic change to your lifestyle that will make your spouse feel more loved.	
Talk about some emotional pain you're experiencing because of a friendship.		Admit to a loss that is making you sad (See Megazone P120-123)		Ask your spouse to grieve with you over something you have lost. (See Megazone P120-123)	

At the end of the week write about whether you succeeded or have the potential to succeed and how it's making you feel.

Photography: Sue Roseblade

Wastefulness or Wealth

Message

Wastefulness and wealth are intrinsically linked by their apparent opposition to one another. Perhaps it seems unlikely that someone who is wasteful will become wealthy or that someone wealthy is likely to be a wasteful individual, but of course there are exceptions. For Mr and Mrs Average keeping the monthly outgoings under budget is a tricky juggling act and can often be the trigger of the most volatile disagreements within a marriage.

"Whether the wife purchases an expensive camera or the husband a new golf club is not the core issue in what can become a monumental fight, but rather the deeper attitude toward what money means, how it should be spent and whether the financial interests of the couple are more important than indulging an individual whim. Similarity in core values serves as a form of inoculation against fighting and arguing."

Karl Pillemer, 30 Lessons for Living

"It doesn't matter how much money the other person makes. If you don't share core values, your relationship will likely be tenuous at best."

www.todaysquotefromgod.com 19/8/2014.

These two pearls of wisdom highlight the need to sit down and talk about how we use our money, not just once, but on a regular basis. What one of us thinks of as value for money, the other may well consider wasteful. What one of us would like to give away the other may want to save. We need to talk and we need to agree on some set principles, even rules, which will make us both feel comfortable.

Meditation

Consider the wisdom of these words:

"Discipline is wisdom and vice versa." Scott Peck

"Money often costs too much." Ralph Waldo Emerson

Think for a moment about the emotions that the thought of money creates in you:
happiness / excitement / fear / anxiety / sadness / jealousy / guilt / other:

Mission "Look After the Pennies"

W

WEEK 1: Your mission is to consider to what extent you are wasteful with money, time and possessions. We could all make some adjustments to refine our use of resources. Take a few minutes to pick out some changes you could make that would bless and encourage your husband or wife:

How I could improve my use of.....

MONEY	TIME	POSSESSIONS

Share your completed charts with each other and agree what first steps you will each take this week.

WEEK 2: Your mission is to review your wealth and come to a joint agreement on how it is used. Before you try this activity, if you think it may cause difficulty or argument between you, visit www.marriagebuilders.com and read Dr Harley's 'Policy of Joint Agreement'. Discuss how it could be helpful to you to adopt the policy in relation to your financial decisions.

Take turns to answer these questions honestly. Make sure you have each said everything you would like to say before moving on to the next question. If there is a long road ahead of you, just tackle one or two questions and make a plan for a few small first steps towards improvement:

1. Do you need outside help to sort out your finances? If so are you willing to find some together?

2. To what extent do you feel your finances are a source of conflict between you?

3. What needs to happen to make you feel happier about the way your money is used?

4. How happy are you with your work and/or the role you are currently playing in bringing income into the marriage?

5. Does your money make you feel closer as a couple or more distant? Why? What needs to change?

6. What are your outgoings each month and what spare cash is available, if any?

7. Are you keeping a close enough eye on the budget, and whose responsibility should that be?

8. What future financial goals would you most like to be working towards?

9. Do you handle your use of credit cards well?

10. Are you both completely transparent with each other when it comes to your spending?

For further help from an outside agency or to join an excellent course on budgeting check out: www.capmoney.org

Micro Story

Steven: "We decided when we were first married to keep our separate bank accounts. We were both earning a reasonable wage and enjoyed the freedom of deciding how to spend our spare cash. I paid the bills and Helen paid the mortgage. It seemed to work fine. We expected it to change when she stopped work to bring up the family, but I wasn't prepared for how it would make me feel.

I put a proportion of my salary into her account each month so that she could manage the house and the children's needs, but I couldn't help myself keeping mental records of ways in which I thought she was being wasteful or reckless. I would confront her whenever she bought gifts for friends, or went out for coffee. I knew I was envious of the fact that she no longer had to go to work and I know I started taking it out on her with my attitudes. Whenever she asked if we could afford to buy something, I would snap back at her and find a reason that we couldn't. I became suspicious that Helen was buying things that she didn't tell me about and would snoop around the house like a burglar trying to prove myself right."

Helen: "When I stopped work I was envious of Steven as he still had the right to spend money on himself, because he was the one earning it. He never said as much, but it was written all over his face if I ever challenged him on some small indulgence he decided he deserved. I felt like a second class citizen in a marriage that had previously been between two equal partners. It wasn't as if we should have been struggling for funds at the end of the month. He'd had several promotions, and the one income was technically enough. Yet it seemed to just drip through our fingers. It was like a silent competition between us. If one of us spent a certain amount, the other would find a reason to spend at least that amount on something they wanted. I started to not tell him when I bought something, so that he wouldn't just go off and waste money to get even with me. That just made me feel really guilty, and yet it became a sort of compulsive habit. After a while, I never even thought to ask him any more before making a purchase."

Steven: "It was only when the girls started at secondary school and Helen went back to work that we finally sat down one evening and found ourselves able to have a conversation about money. Since that night things have improved tremendously. To start with we were treading on eggshells a bit, but we promised each other that we would look at the finances together one evening a month and talk about what we would like to do with the income available. We opened a joint bank account and a savings account and we allocated a set sum that each of us can spend in a month without having to consult the other person. Beyond that amount, we always make joint decisions on where the money goes. Without that turn around, I don't think we would still be married. Looking back, the relationship had reached some very rocky ground. But now we can trust each other and that feels good."

W

Eight year old Ava's advice for marriage preparation:

"Make sure at least one of you knows how to do online banking, because however much you love each other, the bills have still got to be paid!"

©iStockphoto.com/tereeez

Myth Or Truth?

".....the love of money is the root of all evils....." 1 Timothy 6:10 RSV

"If the grass looks greener on the other side of the fence, it's because they take better care of it." Cecil Selig

Photography: Sue Roseblade

X-pectations & X-cuses

Message

An expectation, according to the Oxford Dictionary, has two definitions. Firstly it is a strong belief that something will happen. Secondly it is a belief that someone will or should achieve something. Expecting our spouse to live up to our imaginary ideals will lead us to make unhealthy judgments about them. We need to recognise that we are all on the same journey towards maturity and to give each other time and space to change as we react and respond to all the different things life throws at us. Instead of living with an attitude that our spouse should live up to our expectations, it is far better to live with expectancy. Expectations and expectancy are different. The dictionary says that expectancy is the state of thinking or hoping that something, especially something good, will happen. This relieves the pressure on the other person to perform. It is the attitude by which everything that comes your way feels like a bonus and which leads to spontaneity and overflow in a relationship. It exonerates the other person from failure, because there is no bar to reach. Expectations, on the other hand, can lead to disappointment and stagnation because there is a bar, and it is often unrealistically high.

In order to manage our expectations, it is important to find out whether we share certain key priorities and values, preferably early on in a relationship. Have you ever asked each other whether you believe the same things in life are important? As well as the big and important issues that we hold, most of us have many subconscious expectations of our husband or wife in the comings and goings of our daily routine. We expect to be picked up from work, or to have a meal put in front of us. Perhaps we expect certain standards of cleanliness around the home, or to have the other person sweep the leaves or change the light bulbs. Maybe we expect to watch whatever we want on TV or to make love a certain number of times a month. We cannot live with someone our whole lives and not fall into certain patterns of behaviour that lead to these expectations developing. We can, however, learn to recognise that we do have expectations and begin to protect the relationship from any negative impact they may have had on us in the past.

Often our expectations will let us down through no fault of our husband or wife. If we expect our spouse to stay fit and healthy and they fall sick, we may feel disappointed. If we expect them to earn a large salary and they fail to get promoted, again we can be upset or annoyed at the way things turn out. If we expect that our spouse will outlive us but they die first, our bereavement can be doubly hard to bear. Unrealistic expectations will mean that we experience many more losses in the course of our lifetime, and take them as harder knock backs, than if we live with contentment combined with a sense of expectancy.

Expectations will most likely lead to tension. They can be the trigger for many needless arguments. If one or both of us gets uptight, upset or annoyed over a small matter between us, we are only human if our first reaction is defensive. Often it is genuinely hard to understand that we have done anything wrong. The trouble is that this defensiveness backs us into a corner, and leads to making excuses.

None of us is perfect, but usually most of us could do better. The easy way out is to blame the other person. If, instead of retaliating, we can teach ourselves to have restraint and make our reply softly and kindly without defensiveness, we will cease to alienate one another. Excuses are the immature spouse's alternative for apologies. Train yourself to apologise swiftly and fully, without any condescension in your voice. Give yourself to practising a loving attitude when you feel quite the opposite. Learn that in losing the battle you are winning your spouse's heart and soon you will have no need of your excuses any more.

©FreeImages.com/redster

Meditation

X

Marriage is a covenant. Think for a moment about how that is different from a contract. Would you agree that a covenant works by having aims to strive towards (expectancy), whereas a contract is based on claims (or expectations)?

In a covenant we are interdependent, which means we belong with each other not to each other.

Think about how you can be a help rather than a hindrance to your husband or wife as they aim towards reaching their full potential.

Mission "The X Factor"

WEEK 1: Your mission is to move from x-pectation to x-oneration and x-pectancy.

For each area of life listed in the table below, write down your basic values or principles, then discuss what you have written and work towards some agreed value statements. Here's an example of things you might write, but it will vary from person to person:

Money – ***We should make and keep to a budget, and save up for what we can't afford. I'd like us to only use a credit card if I know we can pay it off at the end of the month. We should have a shared account, but allow each other some individual spending money. I expect us to work towards managing on one income when we are ready to have a family!***

Money

Work

Children

Sex

Chores

Faith

Family

Ambitions

Use of technology

Other:

Now circle any of these examples of smaller issues and daily routines over which you have held expectations and add any of your own:

transport **cooking** **laundry** **friendships** **family time**

good manners **holiday planning** **tidiness** **working hours** **punctuality**

Ask your spouse how they feel about your attitude towards these issues and discuss how you could shift from expectation to exoneration (letting them off the hook) and then move towards a healthier form of expectancy.

Myth Or Truth?

Setting each other free from expectations, enables us to reach our full potential.
If I cannot love myself, how can I expect anyone else to love me?
We need to relinquish our rights whilst retaining our responsibilities.

Micro Stories

We asked people what expectations they had in their marriages and these were some of the responses we received:

Jenny: I realise now that I always expected Ryan to be as family oriented as I was. He said before we got married that he wanted children, but I didn't understand that once we had them, we would each see the commitment to bringing them up very differently. It has been hard working through that.

Sylvie: Maybe it's old fashioned of me, but I expected good manners. I wanted my guy to open doors for me, and introduce me to people at parties..... you know..... the knight in shining armour image..... but it's taken a lot of training, (dare I say nagging - although I try not to) even with things like not talking with his mouth full. I can't bear that!

Kurt: To be brutally honest, I expected my wife, Jenna to be more dynamic in the bedroom. Sex has been a disappointment from day 1. She says I shouldn't go by what I see in films, but it's hard not to have that in the back of your mind. I'm trying to think about her needs and change my expectations, but I have to admit it's not easy.

Damaris: We come from two very different cultures. We got together through an exciting holiday romance which led to us getting married after just 11 months together. Looking back now I see we should have talked more about how our background and upbringing would affect the relationship. I expected John to fit in with my family, but he finds socialising with them terribly difficult. I didn't think he was introverted when we met, but the expectations of my extended family seem to have made him retreat into his shell.

The age old blame game.....

©Rgbstock.com/SisCiel

God said to Adam, "Have you eaten from the tree that I commanded you not to eat from?"

Adam replied, "The woman you put here with me..... she gave me some fruit from the tree, and I ate it."

Genesis 3:11-12

Humza: I expected that we would both work full time. I guess having plenty of money was more important to me. When we had the kids it was hard to be the only one bringing in the wage and I kind of resented handing over my cash for housekeeping and not having any left for myself. I've got over it though, and now I see it as a bonus if I can afford to go to football or out with my mates once in a while.

Marcus: Our issue was the housework. Neither of us like doing the chores and we both expected the other person to be more willing to take a bigger part in getting stuff done. Even though we have split the tasks between us, we can still be quite judgmental if we've done our share, and the other person hasn't got round to doing theirs.

©FreeImages.com/karen andrews

"To eat dust is to feed on your shortcomings and lack, until you constantly feel that there is so much in your life that you need to clean up. You may not be physically bowed over, but you become dust-conscious and life every day is a struggle. Having dust-consciousness affects the way you see others. You look at people's faults all the time. You point out their shortcomings and rake up their past failures. When you are dust-conscious, you find your relationships robbed of peace and joy. If you don't want to be devoured, then lift your eyes above the dust! Instead of looking at your failures, look to Christ who has delivered you from every defeat."

Joseph Prince

WEEK 2: Your mission is to move from x-cuses to x-planations and apologies.

On a scale of 1-10 how good would you say you are at apologising for poor behaviour / wrong attitudes? Ask your spouse if they agree with your estimate!

Discuss the difference between an excuse, an explanation and an apology.

Ask your spouse if there is one thing that has happened in the last week that they would like you to apologise for. When they tell you, follow these 8 steps which will lead you towards reconciliation:

1. Take a moment to check your attitude and to allow a sense of remorse to develop.
2. Gain some self control and decide not to be defensive.
3. Admit you were in the wrong.
4. State fully and precisely what it was you did or said that was wrong.
5. Acknowledge how you think your spouse might be feeling about your behaviour.
6. Present a genuine and heartfelt apology.
7. Specifically ask for your spouse's forgiveness.
8. Acknowledge with thankfulness that you have received their response.

Practise this procedure whenever it becomes necessary in the coming week and determine to give each other a clean slate every day.

Youth & Yesterdays

Message

The media tries its best to persuade us that one of our greatest needs is to stay young for as long as possible. Huge industries are built around people's desire to thwart the ageing process. But if we are taken in by this pressure to conform, we all face fighting a losing battle. We are given the impression, and can be duped into believing, that youth is a more valuable, more important, more precious stage of life than older age. This, alongside the health challenges we may face, can lead us to a lack of appreciation of the benefits of growing older.

Let's not forget the value of gaining wisdom and insight as we age. Often we become more 'comfortable in our own skin' once we are able to leave behind peer pressure and the keeping up of appearances. The making of memories has a significant impact on us which we can review in one of two ways. We can either feel a sense of loss that those times are past and cannot be relived, or we can allow them to feed us and fill us, so that we become rich and mature. This does not so much depend on whether we have good memories or bad ones, but on how we have allowed our experiences to mould and shape us.

A good memory could either lead us to regret that those days have gone, or it could enrich our sense of wellbeing for the joy that has been added to our life. Equally a bad memory could either hold us in grief and pain, or we could work towards a feeling of gratitude that time has moved us on. We have more opportunity for happiness when we are able to let go of the past and live in the present. Bad memories can be useful to us in guiding us away from making the same mistakes again, teaching us better skills and behaviours or protecting us from being similarly endangered again.

Thus, it is good to be able to view our yesterdays not as time lost, but as a bank of experiences gained, which continue with us and enrich our present. The story of Abraham ends with this concept when it describes him as being 'full of years'.

"Then Abraham breathed his last and died at a good old age, an old man and full of years....." Genesis 25:8

Myth Or Truth?

Y

It doesn't matter what is ahead of you, as long as you know who is behind you.

Live for today for tomorrow never comes.

"*Keep young and beautiful, if you want to be loved!*" (title of a song from a 1933 movie called Roman Scandals)

If I had married the ideal Mr or Mrs Right, who must have been out there somewhere, we would have had the perfect 'happy ever after'.

Beauty is more than skin deep. Many of us become more lovable as we age, particularly if we face up to the challenge of character development.

©FreeImages.com/David Basson

"I now think of marriage like I think about living in my home state of Minnesota. You move into marriage in the springtime of hope, but eventually arrive at the Minnesota winter, with its cold and darkness. Many of us are tempted to give up and move south at this point, not realising that maybe we've hit a rough spot in a marriage that's actually above average. The problem with giving up, of course, is that our next marriage will enter its own winter at some point. So do we just keep moving on, or do we make our stand now..... with this person, in this season? That's the moral, existential question we face when our marriage is in trouble." Bill Doherty

©FreeImages.com/Shannon Pifko

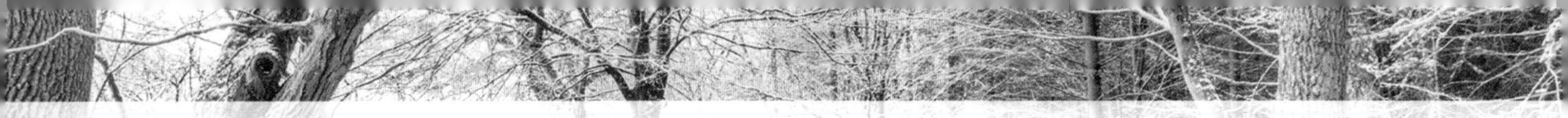

Meditation

What aspect of being young would you most not want to repeat?

Ladies: What words would you use to describe "a real gentleman", in the old fashioned sense of the term?

Gents: How would you describe the difference between a woman and a lady?

©FreeImages.com/Andreas Krappweis

©FreeImages.com/Yamamoto Ortiz

Micro Story

Couples who had reached their golden wedding were asked to say to say how they thought they had changed over the course of 50 years:

Violeta: We learned not to be so excessive about anything. Stephan was always so passionate and threw himself into any new venture without stopping to think about the consequences. Now we take decisions with more reason than emotion.

Lewis: Our love isn't like the passionate fireworks of our twenties any more, but it has been replaced with a great sense of security and there is tremendous comfort in growing old together with the person who knows you better than anyone else.

Stan: Probably we got a bit wiser. We realised we weren't going to achieve all we hoped for, but that in itself has taught us how to live with the disappointment of letting go of dreams.

www.reddit.com (on www.businessinsider.com)

Michael: I wasn't very self-controlled as a young man. I have a bit of colour in my past and I guess I'm glad I left that behind. Mary was quite impetuous too, but in a different way and I guess we helped each other in the end.

Anisha: When I was young I trusted anybody and everybody. Then after some bad experiences, I trusted no one for a time. I had to start over when I met Nitin. I was more cautious, but we have learned to be faithful and loyal to each other.

Lily: It's been an up and down relationship, but we have learned to enjoy each day and to be more gentle with each other.

Albert: We became less hot-headed. We stopped throwing crockery around. It got too expensive!

Mission "Memory Lane"

WEEK 1: Your mission is to set some new goals for your character development.

Think about what you were like as a young person. Make a list of the characteristics you are glad to have left behind and contrast them with qualities that you aspire towards:

Youthful Characteristics	Aspirations for Older Age
Eg: Often sulky when things didn't go my way	*Eg: To express emotions in constructive ways*

Talk with your husband or wife about how you can help each other with these aspirations. Write down one new goal that you would like to set as a priority:

"There is a fine balance between honouring the past and losing yourself in it. For example, you can acknowledge and learn from mistakes you made, and then move on and refocus on the now. It is called forgiving yourself." Eckhart Tolle

WEEK 2: Your mission is to allow your memories to make you 'full of years'.

Look at your old photos and spend an hour together enjoying your memories of the good times.
Plan to make another memory soon.

Zeds or Zest

Message

If you have been faithfully working through the magazine in alphabetical order: congratulations..... you have arrived at the final page! If, on the other hand, you have been dipping in and out at random, by all means enjoy this page now, even though its main purpose is to encourage you to revise and revisit what you have been learning. When you have accomplished all the missions we have set you: well done..... you have just begun! Hopefully, you have gained so much from the depth of connection you've established, that talking about your relationship has become a great habit that you will never want to drop.

So don't set up the zeds once you close THE MAGAZINE for the final time. A relationship is a living entity and it must be fed regularly and watered generously in order to stay alive and well.

Listen to Proverbs 6:6-11 MSG

"You lazy fool, look at an ant.
Watch it closely; let it teach you a thing or two.
Nobody has to tell it what to do.
All summer it stores up food;
At harvest it stockpiles provisions.
So how long are you going to laze around doing nothing?
How long before you get out of bed?
A nap here, a nap there, a day off here, a day off there,
Sit back, take it easy..... do you know what comes next?
Just this: You can look forward to a dirt-poor life,
Poverty your permanent house guest!"

The same principle that applies to our work life also applies to our relationships. Just as a car will run out of fuel and its MOT will expire if we don't pay attention to its needs, so contentment in our marriage today does not mean that we can sit back and set up the zeds for the next week, next month or next year.

Instead, rather than being lazy, we must work at maintaining an enthusiasm for life today and finding the zest that will make our future hopes and dreams into reality. People with such zest for life tend to be among those who prioritise health and fitness as far as possible for the season of life they are in. They also seek out people and projects that make them feel energetic, and they take time out for rest and refreshment. Refuelling our own resource tank is part of the process of keeping love alive, as when we do so, we have plenty to share.

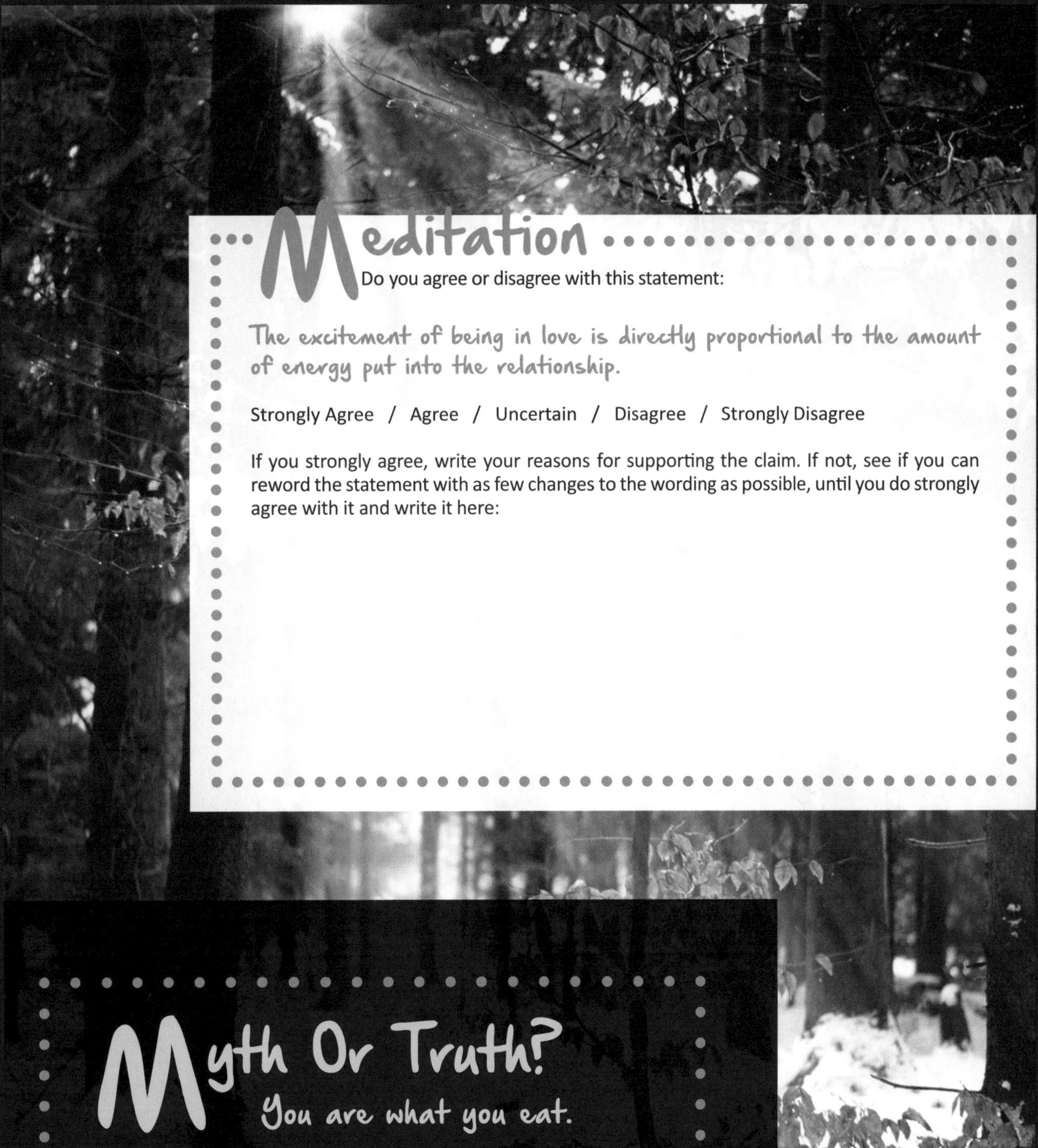

Meditation

Do you agree or disagree with this statement:

The excitement of being in love is directly proportional to the amount of energy put into the relationship.

Strongly Agree / Agree / Uncertain / Disagree / Strongly Disagree

If you strongly agree, write your reasons for supporting the claim. If not, see if you can reword the statement with as few changes to the wording as possible, until you do strongly agree with it and write it here:

Myth Or Truth?

You are what you eat.

"Genius is one percent inspiration, ninety-nine percent perspiration."
Thomas Alva Edison

Hard work never did anyone any harm.

Procrastination is the thief of time.

©FreeImages.com/Andreas Krappweis

©FreeImages.com/Yamamoto Ortiz

Micro Stories

Charlie: "As a teenage lad I used to laugh a lot at Homer Simpson. I had a lot of sympathy for him too! I didn't consciously plan to become like him, although there were many times that I spent 'lazy' weekends on the sofa watching sport when we were first married. I would completely ignore my wife's hints about chores that needed doing when she went off to do her weekend shifts, and even when the kids came along I didn't improve much. I would just leave them doing their own thing as much as possible, so I could do mine.

I didn't set out to be lazy. I just grew up with the same mindset I had seen in my Dad. He came home from the office believing he had done his work. He believed that being the breadwinner was his only responsibility. I would think to myself that my wife's lists weren't urgent; she just didn't like the idea of me relaxing when she was out. I never thought about all the extra things she coped with, even though she worked as many hours as I did.

Before I'm pelted with rocks and tomatoes let me say that I've seen the error of my ways!

When I thought my wife was nagging, and criticising me as a person, my reaction was to ignore her pleas for help. But since we have invested in some counselling, I have learned that she was more desperate than critical. In return, she has learned to ask me for help in a straightforward, unapologetic way, rather than hinting or being sarcastic. Has this totally cured me of my lazy ways? No, but it has helped."

Charlie

Ilvia: "I was slim and quite sporty when we first got together. We had three children in the first seven years of our marriage and each time I found it harder to lose the weight I'd gained during pregnancy. My husband made it obvious in many subtle ways that he found me less attractive than before, and I got more and more depressed. Comfort eating became both my friend and my enemy. The more he turned away from me because of my increasing size, the more I would eat. I never meant to get fat; it was a reaction to my general emotional state and my feelings of rejection in particular. Eventually, at the suggestion of a friend, I went for some counselling. It has taken two years of disciplined diet and exercise, with no magic wand, to get my figure back along with a new zest for life and a renewed marriage as well!"

Ilvia

©FreeImages.com/Michael & Christa Richert

Z

"A successful marriage requires falling in love many times, always with the same person."

Mignon McLaughlin

Mission "Zipping it Up"

WEEK 1: Your mission is to recognise any potential for laziness in your life.

Rate yourself on a scale of 1-10 for the way you devote yourself to each of the following responsibilities. Then rate your husband or wife and finally see if your scores agree!

Responsibility:	**Me**	**You**	**My Totals**
Keeping on top of your own chores			
Offering help beyond scope of your own chores			
Communicating feelings			
Giving loving physical touch			
Making complimentary comments			
Being attentive in conversation			
Dealing with paperwork / bills			
General tidiness			
Being generous with gifts or finances			
Paying sensible attention to your diet			
Putting effort into keeping fit			
Planning for time together			

Add together the score you gave yourself, with the score your spouse gave you in their book for each of the 12 responsibilities, to arrive at a realistic rating out of 20. For example: If you rated yourself 5 out of 10 for keeping on top of your own chores and your spouse rated you at 7 out of 10, that would give you a total score of 12 out of 20.

Choose one of your lowest scoring responsibilities and focus this week on raising your game in that area.

WEEK 2: Your mission is to decide on your future commitment to maintaining an exciting love relationship with your spouse.

Discuss with each other:

a) How you have felt about working through THE MAGAZINE together?

b) What has been the most helpful aspect of THE MAGAZINE for you?

c) What you think you should do to continue to invest in the relationship?

There are some suggestions for further investment in the resources section of The Megazone which you might like to consider.

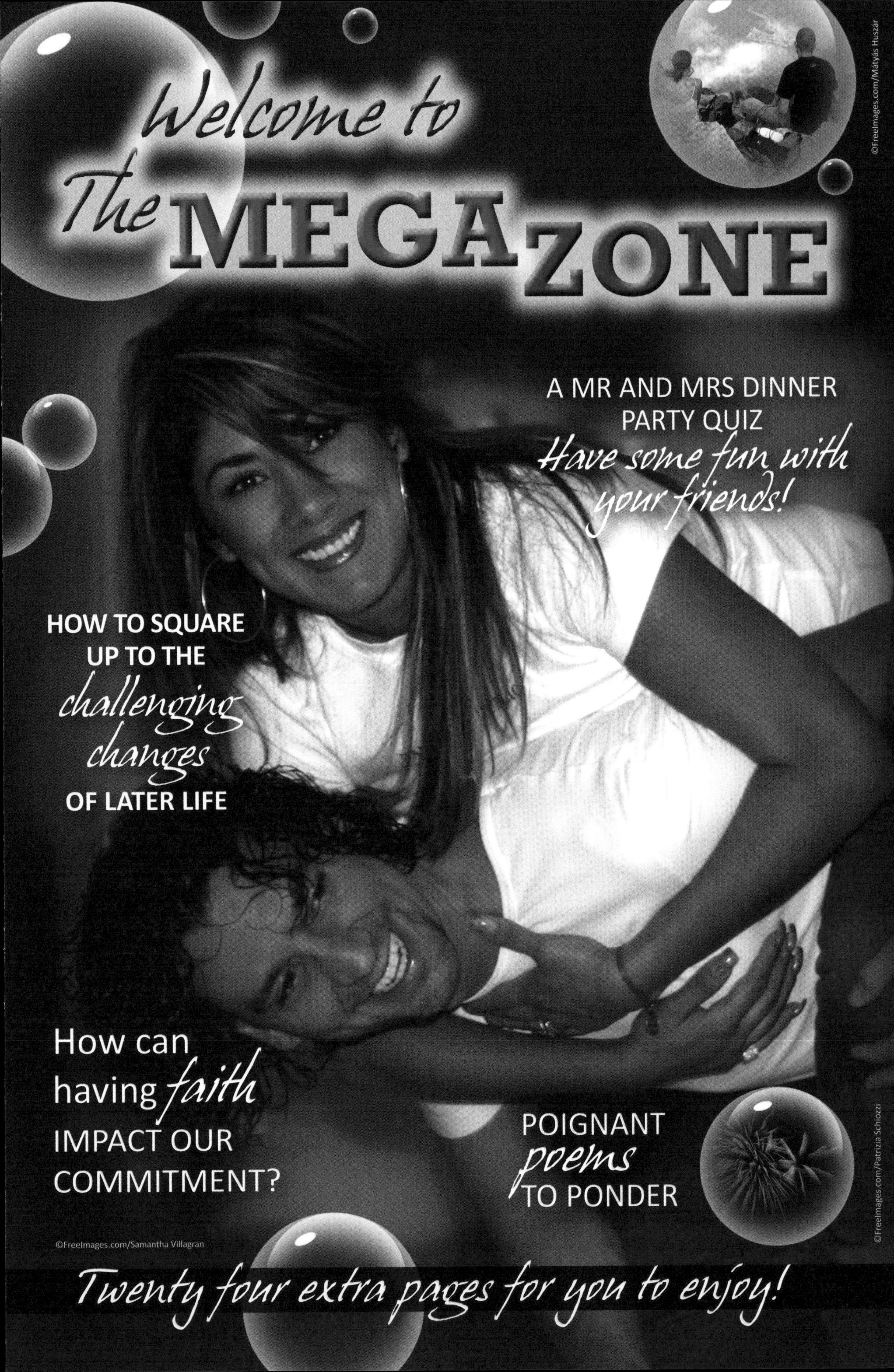
Welcome to
The MEGA ZONE
A MR AND MRS DINNER PARTY QUIZ
Have some fun with your friends!
HOW TO SQUARE UP TO THE challenging changes OF LATER LIFE
How can having faith IMPACT OUR COMMITMENT?
POIGNANT poems TO PONDER
Twenty four extra pages for you to enjoy!
©FreeImages.com/Mátyás Huszár
©FreeImages.com/Patrizia Schiozzi
©FreeImages.com/Samantha Villagran

Alphabetical Adventures

Work together to create a list of fun things you could do together, each one beginning with a different letter of the alphabet! Then see how many of them you can do within the next year!

Hot Chocolate

A

Hiking

darts

B

C

city break

D

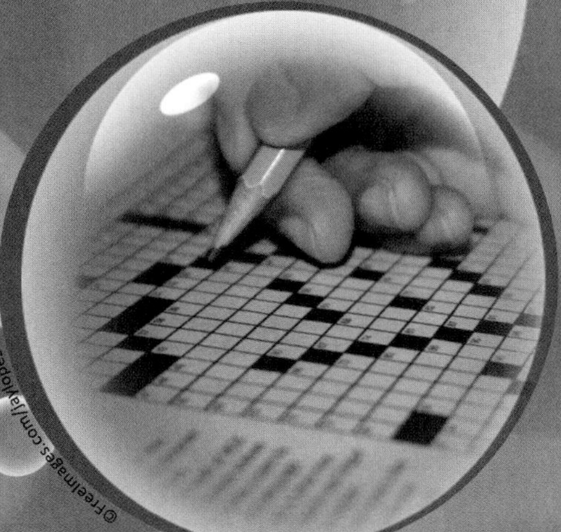

F

E

SWIMMING

©FreeImages.com/ilker
©iStockphoto.com/Xavier Arnau
Continued...
©iStockphoto.com/imagospot

Volunteering
M
N
karaoke
crosswords
O
P
Q
©FreeImages.com/Giuseppe C
museum
©iStockphoto.com/Xavier Arnau
R
S
©FreeImages.com/Stuart Bell
LINE DANCING

T
badminton
U
©FreeImages.com/Tom Pickering
V
W
art gallery
X
picnic
Z
©FreeImages.com/wookie ewok
Y
©iStockphoto.com/imagospot

Sex Starts in Her Head

Men like to look at women; that's a documented fact,
But it's ever been mysterious how a lady may react.....
Embarrassed or disdainful, perhaps flattered or amused,
From the glare of rapt attention she prefers to be excused.

Yet she seeks to be alluring, this creature in her skirts
And watches how her hunter marks her beauty as he flirts.
For it's the chase that lights her fire and, though she wants to be the prize,
She prolongs the courtship ritual for the look that's in his eyes.

Wild thoughts of being captured and protected above all
Heighten sense and defy reason, make her confident, walk tall.
His promise of commitment is what she longs to hear.....
To know he'd climb or run or fight or die to conquer all her fear.

No, this is no children's fairy tale to be mockingly dismissed,
A pure romantic fantasy, or vainly abstract tryst.
The very stuff of life, by which her brain's creatively been wired,
Makes members of the fairer sex so yearn to be desired.

Her elaborate adornment may belie her true agenda.
She wants her outward beauty to entice him to be tender,
But the fragrant invitation of her dress, her talk, her smile,
Has power over nature to unwittingly beguile.

To be known and understood, to be listened to and heard,
To be accepted, loved and valued, and affirmed with deed and word,
Are for a girl prerequisites to passion being fired
And will stop her circuit breakers tripping because of how she's wired.....

For the female brain churns overtime left to its own devices:
Circumventing problems or working through a crisis.
So before a knight in shining armour plans to lead his bride to bed
He needs to know and take account.....
that the sex starts in her head.

Challenging Changes

"If the idea of grieving together is a new concept for you, try it out next time something little goes wrong."

Every one of us lives with the necessity of change throughout the entire course of our life. Some of us embrace changes and actively seek out new experiences; others of us dread the prospect of the status quo being upset. This is understandable, as not all changes will be for better; some will be for worse. In fact, as we get older the balance will gradually shift as we begin to have to accept and come to terms with the concept of loss.

Hoping for changes that will improve our experience of life is normal and natural. Learning to watch and wait for those changes to occur can be challenging. In the context of a relationship most of us find it easier to see how life would improve through changes in our spouse's behaviour, without being able to spot how our own habits and reactions play similarly into the equation. It can be surprising to discover that the best way to achieve a desired outcome is to change ourselves, because then our spouse will more easily begin to change as well.

However, we can often resort to nagging, criticising or manipulating, rather than looking at our own shortcomings, but these unhelpful tactics make it even harder for our spouse to change. We are shooting ourselves in the foot. If, instead, we can continue to act lovingly towards them, and try to understand why they behave as they do, we will develop the patience that can help us to see the situation in a different light.

In effect, given time, I have often seen that the problem becomes the solution because it changes me for the better as I grapple with it!

Frequently couples will clash because one of them wants a change in circumstances, with which the other doesn't agree. Hopefully many of the activities we have prepared for you in THE MAGAZINE will help you to discuss and resolve your disagreements: at least in as far as your differences involve choices that you are free and able to make. However, the type of challenging changes that we want to spend a little more time on in this extra section is those that are thrust upon us, through restrictive circumstances, loss and grief. It wouldn't be right, much as we love being excited, energetic and enthusiastic about life, to pretend that every problem can be overcome, sidestepped or laughed out of court.

Unless we both live to be about 100 years old, we are definitely now in the second half of our marriage, and already facing some of these changes. Although we have been fortunate not to have suffered any major life changing traumas thus far, we know that many couples will have to face tragedy or torment of various kinds even in their early years of relationship. Often the storms of life brew over us due to different types of loss. We can lose possessions, homes, jobs or income stream, loved ones, opportunities, health and strength, savings, pension

expectations, fertility, sexual function or satisfaction, peace, security, friends, purpose, eyesight or hearing, respect, pets, freedom, the ability to drive, get out and about or go for walks and so on. The list could go on. Losses are to be expected throughout our early years as well as later in life, but they can certainly pile up and increase in intensity as we get older.

For our relationship to continue to thrive, or even just to survive, in its latter stages, we need to work out how we can go about grieving these losses together, so that they draw us close rather than pushing us apart. It is much easier to stay in love when all is going well than when times get tough, unless we use our vulnerability to allow us to develop a deeper oneness: and so you see again how the problem can, in and of itself, become the solution.

Have you sometimes been surprised by hearing that a couple who have been together thirty, forty or even fifty years are splitting up? Why, if they have stuck together for all those years, through thick and thin, would they choose to grow old apart? Well maybe, the answer is right there in the question: it's just that there is a lot more thin than thick as we age. If they are not able to help each other to cope with the "thin" times, it may sadly be easier to face those days alone. Getting old isn't for the faint-hearted. It's happening to all of us and, only if we don't bury our heads in the sand now, will we be able to respond to each other in the difficult times ahead with fortitude and grace. For example, it takes so much more patience than we needed in our early years to endlessly repeat ourselves because our loved one has grown deaf or forgetful. For us, now that our children have grown and flown, our great desire is to grow old in a way that gives them courage and confidence to handle whatever challenges they too may face in due course.

Expressing our emotions well is part of the process of working through our losses. If you don't tell people how you are feeling, they cannot comfort you. The word comfort comes from the root words com (with) and fort (strength). It literally means to add strength to a situation. It is the gift we give to people when we share their pain. By adding strength to their emotional resources, they feel better.

Knowing that there is a marked difference between men and women in the ways they express emotion, and that in general women cry much more easily and more frequently than men, we recognise that there is an inherent difficulty with comforting one another. Tears may historically be seen as a weakness in a couple's relationship. Many wives complain that when they cry their husbands switch off from trying to understand them, thinking it's a tactic women use to get their own way. Because explaining emotions in words doesn't necessarily come easily, men can often be tempted to

Continued...

Challenging Changes

Continued...

give up and to think that women are complicated. Women will often give in to tears of frustration and think that men are hard and unfeeling just because they don't dissolve into tears at every twist and turn. With that as a backdrop to the stand off which occurs in many relationships, sometimes it is hard to express grief through tears, because we have become conditioned by our experience that tears bring separation between us, rather than increasing oneness.

Crying by oneself is by definition a lonely and therefore not always a positive experience, although it can be a better option than bottling up our feelings. However, by contrast, with the comfort of someone we love alongside us, crying will usually have a positive effect in helping to clear away the pain caused by our grief. In times of deep sorrow or great loss it will be an intermittent process that we will need to return to over a period of time before we are able to recover. If we can turn to each other and talk about our pain without being rejected, we will heal more quickly and without having to harden our hearts in our attempt to find resilience.

If the idea of grieving together is a new concept for you, try it out next time something little goes wrong. It is good to get acquainted with skills you may well need later on in life.

Here are some steps you could take towards sharing each other's pain:

1. Talk to your spouse about what has happened and say how it has made you feel.

2. Invite them to say how they feel about the fact that you are:
sad / upset / lonely / angry etc.

3. Recognise that you may each express your sadness in different ways and tell each other what kind of emotional response you need to make to the situation.

4. Ask for the kind of comfort and support that you would like your spouse to give you and offer what they ask for from you.

5. Check in with each other at frequent intervals, asking how things are going and allow for further intermittent expressions of grief and comfort over time.

If you have unresolved issues from the past, over which you were not able to grieve together at the time, these steps can still be very helpful if used retrospectively.

Sue

The Female of the Species

When the Himalayan peasant meets the he-bear in his pride,
He shouts to scare the monster, who will often turn aside.
But the she-bear thus accosted rends the peasant tooth and nail.
For the female of the species is more deadly than the male.

When Nag the basking cobra hears the careless foot of man,
He will sometimes wriggle sideways and avoid it if he can.
But his mate makes no such motion where she camps beside the trail.
For the female of the species is more deadly than the male.

When the early Jesuit fathers preached to Hurons and Choctaws,
They prayed to be delivered from the vengeance of the squaws.
'Twas the women, not the warriors, turned those stark enthusiasts pale.
For the female of the species is more deadly than the male.

Man's timid heart is bursting with the things he must not say,
For the woman that God gave him isn't his to give away;
But when hunter meets with husbands, each confirms the other's tale—
The female of the species is more deadly than the male.

Man, a bear in most relations—worm and savage otherwise,
man propounds negotiations, man accepts the compromise.
Very rarely will he squarely push the logic of a fact
To its ultimate conclusion in unmitigated act.

Fear, or foolishness, impels him, 'ere he lay the wicked low,
To concede some form of trial even to his fiercest foe.
Mirth obscene diverts his anger—doubt and pity oft perplex
Him in dealing with an issue—to the scandal of the sex!

But the woman that God gave him, every fibre of her frame
Proves her launched for one sole issue, armed and engined for the same;
And to serve that single issue, lest the generations fail,
The female of the species must be deadlier than the male.

She who faces Death by torture for each life beneath her breast
May not deal in doubt or pity—must not swerve for fact or jest.
These be purely male diversions—not in these her honour dwells—
She the other law we live by, is that law and nothing else.

She can bring no more to living than the powers that make her great
As the mother of the infant and the mistress of the mate.
And when babe and man are lacking and she strides unclaimed to claim
Her right as femme (and baron), her equipment is the same.

She is wedded to convictions—in default of grosser ties;
Her contentions are her children, heaven help him who denies!
He will meet no suave discussion, but the instant, white-hot, wild,
Wakened female of the species warring as for spouse and child.

Unprovoked and awful charges—even so the she-bear fights,
Speech that drips, corrodes, and poisons—even so the cobra bites,
Scientific vivisection of one nerve till it is raw
And the victim writhes in anguish—like the Jesuit with the squaw!

So it comes that man, the coward, when he gathers to confer
With his fellow-braves in council, dare not leave a place for her
Where, at war with life and conscience, he uplifts his erring hands
To some God of abstract justice—which no woman understands.

And man knows it! Knows, moreover, that the woman that God gave him
Must command but may not govern—shall enthral but not enslave him.
And she knows, because she warns him, and her instincts never fail,
That the female of her species is more deadly than the male.

Rudyard Kipling (1865-1936)

Gravity and Groundwork

This page is for those of you who are curious, puzzled or freaked out by the idea that God would have anything to do with your relationship, but you are interested in thinking it through. If it isn't for you, then skip it for now. Come back to it when you need to. Most of us deal with the questions it raises at some point in our lives. It takes courage to face the message. It takes more courage to ignore it!

Ryan Frederick of www.fiercemarriage.com puts the challenge to us on his web page.....

Someone asked me the other day, "If you could have coffee with every young couple who reads your blog, what would you say to them?"

The question caught me off guard and I didn't know how to answer them right away. After a few days of hashing through quick responses, I kept coming up short. I felt that if I had ONE opportunity I'd want to find the perfect topic.

I considered topics like communication, commitment, honesty, intimacy, etc. All are important aspects of marriage, but anything we'd discuss along those lines would only address behaviours.

I realised that behaviours don't just materialise from thin air. Behaviours are born somewhere. All behaviour stems from belief and until you change your belief, you'll always gravitate back to your original behaviours. Why else did Paul talk about "renewing your mind" (Romans 12:1-2) and becoming a "new creation" (2 Corinthians 5:17)?

So, if I could sit down with you and talk about anything, I'd discuss your beliefs. Grab some coffee, pull up a chair, and let's talk.....

The Gravity of Belief

Every expectation, behaviour, and consideration for your marriage begins with your beliefs. Think of belief as gravity and your behaviour as a rock. You are charged with keeping the rock in flight. You can throw the rock up but it will fall back to the ground. If you're feeling tenacious, you can build a contraption that launches the rock five miles into the sky. You could even engineer some wings and a rocket to make it fly. With a lot of work, a ton of scheming, and boatloads of fuel, you may be able to make it fly for an hour or two.

©FreeImages.com/Leszek Soltys

In all cases, the rock will inevitably return to the earth.

Every. Single. Time.

Now, what if your life depended on keeping the rock in the air forever? You'd be out of luck pretty quick; it's an impossible task.
Now, what if the rock weighed 5lbs? How about 20lbs? 1000lbs? The heavier the rock, the lower your chances for success.

Unless.....

Unless you turned gravity upside down. Unless everything changed.

You see where I'm going with this. Real change starts in your heart. And real heart change starts with your beliefs. The heavier the burden of your actions, the more necessary heart change becomes. And as you likely know, marital issues can get very heavy...

Now we're talking

So the big questions become "what do you believe?" and "what should you believe?" How you answer those huge questions will determine how you act and why you act the way you do. How about a few granular questions to flesh it out – in no particular order:
(I encourage you and your partner to consider these and write down your answers)

1. What is love? How do you show it? What does it require?

2. Who are you? Who are you as a human being? What is your worth? What is your nature?

3. What is the purpose of marriage? What is your purpose as an individual?

4. Who is God? Who is Jesus?

5. Is the Bible God's sovereign Word? Does it have authority in your life and your marriage? Why?

6. What determines what's right or wrong? What about grey areas?

In case you're wondering, these are not rhetorical questions. What do you actually believe?

What if your spouse doesn't meet your expectations sexually? What should you even expect when it comes to sex? What happens if you feel legitimately wronged? What if you don't feel like forgiving?

See, everything you do stems from these big questions about belief.
To make things more complicated, the questions posed above are not questions you can find answers for without faith. You must anchor yourself in some belief or they'll never be answered. Everyone believes in something. **Everyone.**

Quick sidebar: Last year I wrote an essay on the philosophy of belief. In 2300 words I reached the conclusion that everyone believes – yes, even atheists and agnostics. I'm not the only person to reach this conclusion, and I'm certainly not the first (or the smartest). The evidence is strong: everyone, at their core, chooses to believe something. Not everyone, however, is equally honest about their propensity for belief.

Now, instead of asking whether you believe in something or not, the question becomes one of what you believe.

You'll find a list of what we believe on p129. Though not every line explicitly mentions marriage, every bit of our marriage flows from our core beliefs. Selena and I know and agree on each statement deeply–in our guts. There's no doubt in our minds that when issues arise in our marriage, we have to lean into everything we believe to find a solution.

©FreeImages.com/Alla Leitus

> If you believe marriage is meant for your happiness, you'll waiver in your commitment as soon as happiness eludes you. Is unhappiness enough reason to give up? If you're like most, you're probably thinking "absolutely not". But what about the next time you feel genuinely unsatisfied and frustrated?

Continued...

Gravity and Groundwork

Continued...

©FreeImages.com/Charlie Balch

Our list below reflects core Christian doctrines. This is what we believe, it's who we are, and Jesus is the only reason we're still married. I definitely encourage you to sit down with your spouse and discuss your core beliefs.

We believe:

- the Scriptures are true, authoritative and sufficient.
- there is only one true God, Creator of heaven and earth, who eternally exists in three distinct persons: Father, Son and Holy Spirit.
- all things exist for the glory of God– including us, including the institution of marriage.
- we are sinful by both birth and action.
- the deserved penalty for sin is physical and spiritual death.
- Jesus Christ is the eternal Son of God, was born of a virgin and is both fully God and fully human.
- Jesus Christ died as the sacrificial substitute to pay the penalty for sin.
- Jesus Christ physically rose from the dead, ascended into heaven and will one day physically return.
- there will be a future physical resurrection of the dead. Only those who turn from sin and to Jesus in faith and repentance will be raised to eternal reward. Those who do not turn from sin and to Jesus will be raised to eternal punishment.
- only through faith in the person and work of Jesus Christ and repentance from sin can one be reconciled to God and experience true life and joy.
- that marriage is a lifelong covenant between one man and one woman.
- the relationship between husband and wife should mirror the relationship between Christ and the church.
- as part of God's good order, husbands and wives are to have different yet complementary roles and responsibilities. Men and women are of equal value, worth, and importance in the eyes of God, and should be viewed as such by all.

As I've stated, every bit of our marriage flows from these core beliefs. It's impossible for us to deal with any meaningful part of our marriage without them.

I sincerely hope you also believe these things; Jesus Christ literally means the world to us. If you do believe in Jesus, I hope you take some time and explicitly articulate your Biblical beliefs in your household. Belief statements like these need not be restricted to church websites and official doctrinal statements. Make sure you know for yourself what it means to follow Christ and place your faith in him.

Ryan Frederick

www.fiercemarriage.com

©iStockphoto.com/Annett Vauteck

©iStockphoto.com/mauro grigollo

©iStockphoto.com/Razvan

©iStockphoto.com/AndreyPopov

Shall We Dance?

Understanding romance is a challenge to us guys,
Because our ladies' moods and fancies can take us by surprise;
The treat of topmost value from last week, last month, last year,
Has now fallen out of favour (though not so with us and beer)!!!

If a new idea is needed, a new gift, a new approach,
And our trusty list is failing, where can we find a coach,
Who will help us solve the mysteries that surround this tricky dance,
And unlock the strange enigma that's been labelled as romance?

Is it made of pink and fluffy stuff? Is it delicious, warm or sweet?
Does it matter what it cost us? Must it be nice to smell or eat?
Is it wrapped in pretty paper, tied with curly ribbon tails?
Is it colour for her hair or lips, or polish for her nails?

When we try our best to please; with chocolates, flowers and wine,
When we take her out for coffee or find a special place to dine,
When we help around the house doing chores we really hate,
Or we run a bath, light candles or arrange surprising dates.....

What is it that's still lacking? How have we missed the mark?
What elusive last ingredient still keeps us in the dark?
Come close and study earnestly, your coach is her own heart;
She longs to share her hopes and dreams – with you, her counterpart.

No other coach is needed, if you will but pay attention.
Don't dismiss, sideline or once ignore a thing you hear her mention,
For entering her world is to give both ear and due response,
And frequently will hit the spot: for her this is romance.

©iStockphoto.com/ncognet0

©iStockphoto.com/tetmc

©iStockphoto.com/nikkytok

©iStockphoto.com/Ales_Utovko

©iStockphoto.com/Stas Perov

On the face of it so simple, and yet complicated too.....
If we have our own agenda, or a different point of view,
We're on our guard immediately, afraid of arguments we'll lose,
So we give the silent treatment, or escape however we may choose.....

And then we feel offended that our efforts all fall flat;
She doesn't seem enamoured by little treats of this or that.
We think we know the formula (which steps make up the dance),
But we're filtering out the heartbeat that would help us with our stance.

So don't presume to know her: good questions are the key.
Ask how things have made her feel, what problems she can see.
Show her that you want to serve, but ask what matters most;
It's no good making coq-au-vin if all she wants is toast!!!

And finally a tip for putting icing on the cake;
Learn to express your heart to her, with kindness, nothing fake.
She reads you like a book and knows the things you think and feel,
But returning her heart's openness is somehow the real deal.

Whilst acknowledging the mystery, look beyond it to the key;
It's in your hands to solve it with the gift of honesty.
Assess if you're ignoring things that ought to be addressed,
And start the conversation, giving every ounce your best.

Salsa, Tango, Charleston, Rock'n'Roll may pass you by,
If, two left feet notwithstanding, you're just not that ballroom guy.
But now you've learned the secret at the heart of great romance,
You can go hot foot and pop the question,

*"Hey Baby,
Shall we dance?"*

Rolls Royce Relationships

More Wise Words and Quality Quotations

“They say it takes a village to raise a child. That may be the case, but the truth is that it takes a lot of solid, stable marriages to create a village.”

Diane Sollee

©FreeImages.com/Tom Romig

“On the girl's brown legs there were many small white scars. I was thinking, Do those scars cover the whole of you, like the stars and the moons on your dress? I thought that would be pretty too, and I ask you right here please to agree with me that a scar is never ugly. That is what the scar makers want us to think. But you and I, we must make an agreement to defy them. We must see all scars as beauty. Okay? This will be our secret. Because take it from me, a scar does not form on the dying. A scar means, I survived.”

Chris Cleave, Little Bee

“The secret to having a good marriage is to understand that marriage must be total, it must be permanent, and it must be equal.”

Frank Pittman

Giving a calm explanation of the reasons behind our negative feelings can be the trigger that helps to overcome them.

When we take control of our reactions to our feelings, our husband or wife will not feel blamed and will therefore be more likely to understand and empathise.

Don't rub it in, rub it out!!!

Submission doesn't mean that you can't express your point of view. It does mean you won't enforce it.

©FreeImages.com/Sepas Mohammadpour

"Being heard is so close to being loved that for the average person, they are almost indistinguishable."
David Augsburger

"Don't just follow your heart because your heart can be deceived..... but LEAD your heart."
Fireproof, The Movie

"When someone loves you, the way they talk about you is different. You feel safe and comfortable."
Jess C. Scott, The Intern

"A couple arguing in public is like the body bleeding, but there are other forms of death that aren't apparent on the outside. People are shocked by cancer, so noiseless and invisible, and by the break-up of couples whose hostility to one another never showed."
Rachel Cusk www.theguardian.com/lifeandstyle/2012/feb/17/rachel-cusk-divorce-the-aftermath

©FreeImages.com/Maarten Kruit

"In a futile attempt to erase our past, we deprive the community of our healing gift. If we conceal our wounds out of fear and shame, our inner darkness can neither be illuminated nor become a light for others."
Brennan Manning, Abba's Child: The Cry of the Heart for Intimate Belonging

"The most important thing a father can do for his children is to love their mother."
Theodore Hesburgh

Rolls Royce Relationships
More Wise Words and Quality Quotations Continued...

“Scars are not injuries, Tanner Sack. A scar is a healing. After injury, a scar is what makes you whole.”

China Miéville, The Scar

©FreeImages.com/Mariló González

“Being humble is not a matter of pretending to be worthless, but is a form of realism, not only regarding the real badness of one’s sins and stupidities and the real depth of one’s dependence on God’s grace, but also regarding the real range of one’s abilities. Humble believers know what they can and cannot do. They note both their gifts and their limitations, and so are able to avoid both the unfaithfulness of letting their God-given powers lie fallow and the foolhardiness of biting off more than they can chew.”

J.I. Packer, A Passion for Faithfulness: Wisdom From the Book of Nehemiah

“When there is love in a marriage,
there is harmony in the home;
when there is harmony in the home,
there is contentment in the community;
when there is contentment in the community,
there is prosperity in the nation;
when there is prosperity in the nation,
there is peace in the world.”

Chinese proverb frequently quoted by David and Vera Mace

©FreeImages.com/Rajaram R

“Don't be a buzz kill. When your spouse shares something exciting, match their enthusiasm.”
StanCoMarriage

“Love is what you've been through with somebody.”
James Thurber

“When we are listened to, it creates us, makes us unfold and expand.”
Karl Menninger

“My dad always asks my wife, 'Is he treating you right?' It reminds me of my responsibility to be a good husband.”

National Fatherhood Initiative /Why Knot? Handbook

©FreeImages.com/Nicholas Bumgardner

“We need to deliberately focus on the new creature rather than the old, to see the light in people rather than the darkness. Our dark (or shadow) self has no substance except what we and others create by fearing and indulging it. We must help one another to see and to walk in the light.”

Mike Mason, Practising the Presence of People

Either invite two or three other couples to dinner and play a Mr and Mrs Game with these quiz questions, or use them as your own fun date night activity, by just answering them yourselves and comparing notes when you've finished:

1. What's the one thing, apart from you that he/she would save in a fire?
2. What would he/she say is the most embarrassing thing you've ever done?
3. What would you say is his/her most annoying habit?
4. Who would play him/her in a movie of his/her life?
5. What year did you get together?
6. How many times did he/she take his/her driving test?

7. What's his/her favourite meal?
8. What's his/her favourite song?
9. What's the first movie you ever saw together?
10. What's his/her favourite month of the year?
11. Where was he/she born?
12. What colour are his/her eyes?

13. Is he/she a tidy person?
14. Does he/she like cooking?
15. Does he/she like sport?
16. What is his/her favourite TV programme?
17. What was his/her first job?
18. What newspaper does he/she read?

©FreeImages.com/Jorge Oliveira

19. What is his/her favourite place?
20. What will he/she avoid like the plague?
21. Does he/she like children?
22. How does he/she vote?
23. What time of day is he/she at his/her best?
24. How does he/she like to relax?

25. What is his/her greatest fear?
26. What do you wish you knew about him/her?
27. What, in his/her own opinion, is his/her best feature?
28. If he/she could be anyone famous, who would he/she be?
29. What is his/her speciality in the kitchen?
30. Where would he/she most like to go in the world?

©FreeImages.com/Caroline Hoos

©FreeImages.com/Gina C

Acknowledgements

To our great creator, The God and Father of our Lord Jesus Christ, for His creative power and inspiration to set about this project and see it through to completion.....

To Dave, Stephanie and Chloe, for bearing with us, and with each other, in the long weeks and months of the various stages of design and production.....

To all those who have contributed stories and anecdotes from their own struggles and successes.....

To everyone who has attended the MAZE course and given us their highly valued feedback.....

To our immediate family and also our wider Cowplain Evangelical Church and Time for Marriage networks of support and encouragement.....

THANK YOU!

Dedication

We would like to dedicate THE MAGAZINE to the health of marriage in our nation and beyond, to the foundation of family life in our communities and for the benefit of the children who will become the next generation. More specifically we also dedicate it to the longevity of the four marriages (other than our own) in which we want to invest most of all: those of our four children and their spouses, and we would particularly like to make mention of the last of our four to get married, our eldest son - *Adam* and his wife *Zoe* - our youngest "in-law" as they have so aptly completed our own family's

A-Z *of marriage!*